I0528855

Well
Grounded

Well Grounded

*Cultivating Intimacy
with God*

Beth Madison

NORTHEASTERN BAPTIST PRESS

Bennington, Vermont

Well Grounded
Cultivating Intimacy with God
Copyright © 2024 by Beth Madison

Published by Northeastern Baptist Press
            Post Office Box 4600
            Bennington, VT 05201

All rights reserved. No part of this book may be reproduced in any form without prior permission from Northeastern Baptist Press, except as provided for by USA copyright law.

Scripture quotations are taken from various translations and indicated at each reference.

Cover design by Leason Stiles

Softcover ISBN: 978-1-953331-33-5

Soli Deo Gloria

Psalm 37:4 NIRV
Find your delight in the Lord.
Then He will give you everything your heart really wants.

Contents

Acknowledgements

Thank You, God, that You keep calling me to come close, listen, and learn more of Your lavish love. Thank You that You have always stayed in steadfast love, even when I didn't. Thank You for the gifts of today and the not-yet, all to be delighted in with You.

Thank you to my husband, Andy, and parents, Dr. and Mrs. David L. Coffey, for loving Jesus and people so very well with your lives. You are good gifts from our Good God to me and many others every single day.

Deep gratitude for the entire Union University community, especially the Provost's Office and the Research Committee, for the resources and opportunity to explore the ideas in this book. Your encouragement and support have been invaluable and precious to me, as you are. Thank you.

Thank you to Dr. Sharon Norris Elliott (Authorize Me Literary Agency), Hannah Munley (editor), Drs. Blake Brown and Kelvin Moore, and Dr. Mark Ballard and all the great folks at Northeastern Baptist Press. Thank you for your dedication to excellence, beauty, and the spread of the Gospel through all means possible.

INTRODUCTION

...but Jesus said, "Let the little children come to me and do not hinder them, for to such belongs the kingdom of heaven."
Matthew 19:14 ESV

"[Spiritual disciplines are] not merely vertical channels for cultivating our relationship with God but horizontal conduits that direct us into loving what God loves, including our neighbors and God's creation." [1]
J.K.A. Smith

Have you heard of the scientific method? Even if you have, you might not know what it is. Most people, including scientists like me, don't really know what the scientific method truly is, because its definitions can vary widely. No one can fully agree on what it is or isn't, depending on a scientist's training and discipline, which can also vary widely. (On that note, did you know that there were soil scientists before picking up this book?) But one thing does hold true – the crux of the scientific method is asking a question and trying to answer that question. And most times, trying to answer one question leads to another and another and...

Which is exactly how this book came about – this soil scientist asking one question which led to another and another and onwards, until voilà; here we are. The questions in each chapter of this book can't be fully answered outside of directly talking with our Good God in heaven someday. Thus, I'll call them my Eden What-If Questions, for that coming day when I'll see Him face to face. But starting today, the exploration of these and other questions can lead us closer to Him. Questions can help us grow in the wisdom, worship, and wonder of God while giving us a greater awareness of our place, purpose, position, and God's power. For as we grow in those characteristics, we grow in intimacy with Him and His creation. A greater and growing intimacy with my Creator God is the deepest desire of this soil scientist's heart. And since you're here with me in the journey, I'm assuming that you have this same desire: a desire to not be easily satisfied with simple answers, but to keep pressing on and in to know our God in the soil of our souls and to worship Him on our knees on the soil underneath our feet. For there in worship, we can learn more of what God desires of us today.

I'm hoping you will meet with our Good God in worship and work as you go through this book. For this book's purpose is to use questions to enhance incorporating spiritual disciplines into our routines for knowing God more intimately in our everyday lives. And what could be better than seeking God and finding Him to be even more beautiful than we can imagine?

Jesus tells us that He wants us to come as *little children* in Matthew 19:14. And this truth gives me much hope! It's not my credentials as a scientist, professor, Bible study teacher, or 47 years of being a Christian giving me access to answers or intimacy with God. Only Jesus gives me access, as described in Ephesians 3:11b-12 ESV; *Christ Jesus our Lord, in whom we have boldness and access with confidence through our faith in him.* Thank You, Jesus, for your gift for me at Calvary, giving me righteousness, eternal life, and access to God!

Yet as a scientist, I see a new picture in these truths from Matthew 19 and Ephesians 3. A picture of the idea of worship through asking questions of my Creator God. Let's explore this picture a bit. Most babies are the best scientists I know. As you probably know well, babies are always exploring their worlds using the tools they came with – mouths, eyes, hands, feet, and ears. They are always touching, tasting, feeling, and listening, filled with wonder and excitement at discovering their vocal cords, fingers, toes, and anything they can grab hold of to put into their mouths. Like scientists, babies are always conducting experiments.

For an example of such experiments, consider my grandmother's dining room table and matching chairs. All are the perfect height for a toddler's mouth. Thus, all are ringed with tiny teeth marks from my mother, sons, and me (and awaiting my grandbaby girl's contributions). These teeth marks are almost evenly spaced along the edges of the table and chairs. Each mark was a new place to test if it was different in texture, taste, or consistency from the place just a few inches away from where each toddler was previously hanging on against gravity with wobbly legs and pudgy fingers. For a baby, each bite, lick, or poke is a dip into discovering the wonder that is furniture, hair, shoes, toys, carpet, or whatever doesn't move (including sleeping dogs).

Similarly, when we come as *little children*, each question can be a discovering of more of the wonder that is creation and our Creator God. Each bite, lick, or poke into the books of Scripture and nature in search of answers can bring a deeper faith and courage needed to take that next wobbly step of obedience closer to our Good God (see Romans 1:19-20). As importantly, just like babies, we are not left to explore without help, guidance, or protection. We have God alive and at work in us as the Holy Spirit. Scripture tells us this clearly in 1 Corinthians 6:19-20 ESV: *Or do you not know that your body is a temple of the Holy Spirit within you, whom you have from God? You are not your own, for you were bought with a price. So glorify God in your body.* And likewise in Ephesians 4:30 ESV: *And do not grieve the Holy Spirit of God, by whom you were sealed for the day of redemption.*

In the busyness and clamor of my day, I can easily forget or overlook the gift of the Holy Spirit and God's presence. I take for granted the gift of God in my day. For example, the other day, I saw something new in Scripture that was simply beautiful and amazing to me. (Please hear me – I'm not advocating this as anything but an observation from this soil scientist*.) Here's my observation - many years ago, Adam and the patriarchs had God *for* us in His Presence as protector, provider, sustainer, and so much more. Then, roughly two thousand years ago, Mary and others had Emmanuel, God *with* us, in the flesh as Jesus Christ. And then, since Pentecost, as Christians, we have the Holy Spirit, quite literally as God *in* us. All miraculous, all beautiful, all worthy of worship.

Moving onwards in this thought, I also see a similar progression in Eden with Adam. God spoke creation into being – God for us. Then He formed Adam from the soil – a pointing to the Adam to come in Jesus, Emmanuel, God with us. Finally, God breathed life into Adam – the *pneuma*, "the life-breath" of John 1 as reflecting the Holy Spirit, God in us.

That observation made me stop in gratitude yet again for the depth of our Good God's love for Adam, for me, for us. He didn't shut everything down after Adam's sin; He already had a plan for redemption in the sacrifice of our Christ (see Revelation 13:8). He did then what He's doing now. He keeps moving closer in, even and especially during those times when I'm set on moving away from Him. Thank You, God, that You don't give up on me! Thank You that You keep pursuing me in Your relentless love!

At the risk of sounding impertinent (not my intention whatsoever!), I think of the Holy Spirit as the caretaker of the soil of my soul. He is the good farmer who constantly walks the land searching for places needing extra work or care. He watches to guard that which is vulnerable. He waters the dry and fertilizes the lacking. He prunes excess vegetation, removes dead leaves, treats diseases, and ties up drooping vines, all in pursuit of that *30-, 60-, 100-fold harvest* of fruit (as in John 15, Matthew 13, and Galatians 5). He cares and convicts. He encourages and exhorts. He pleads and prays. He leans in and loves. He does all of this so that the soil of my soul might be rich, deep, soft, and kept in place. He doesn't give up, even when I do.

An even more beautiful thought is that the Holy Spirit does the very same for all of us as Christians. He is present, purposeful, and ever-preparing for the plans and the plantings of our Good Creator God in our lives. He is the One prompting me to steadily and seriously evaluate the status of the soil of my soul today. Just like He did yesterday and will do tomorrow. He can and will use seemingly unrelated sources to shed light on the true status of something, not what I think I'm seeing. For example, the other day while reading a technical soil science journal article, I read this sentence, "soil scientists are tasked to help humanity become a more sustaining soil-forming agent".[2] The Holy Spirit then used this sentence to convict me yet again in how I wasn't using my opportunities as a Christian and a soil scientist to honor Him with my life. Our Good God gently showed me ways that too much time in social media, procrastination, not trusting His plans, and other poor choices were eroding obedience, and thus; peace, in my life. And in making these choices, the soil of my soul was being ignored and vulnerable to degradation by sin and thus, not helpful to pointing others to Christ. This conviction prompted a reassessment of my habits as to protect my heart as the wellspring of life (see Proverbs 4:23). He isn't limited to my expectations of where or how I'll see Him at work or to religious sources or certain people. He is gracious to come, stay, and work wherever I am – thanks be to God for His relentless pursuing!

To prepare for these plantings in our lives, like a farmer might do in the spring, the Holy Spirit often uses the spiritual disciplines as implements for preparing the soil of the soul. He must prepare the soil to receive the good seeds of truth for a growth of grace and a harvest of faith. These spiritual disciplines can vary in their usage and timing in my life like farming implements in a field before, during, and after a growing season. For example: the Holy Spirit can use repentance to plow and prayer to disk;[3] compassion to irrigate and perseverance to cultivate; and gratitude to fertilize and meditation to plant. He uses these and other vital implements for preparation, change, and growth in the soil of my soul. Just as a farmer considers soil and crop types, climate, landscape position, available resources, and other influences on the desired harvest in his choice of implement usage, the Holy Spirit does the same with me. He intimately knows the soil of my soul, my temperament, inclinations, likes and dislikes, fears, current and past circumstances, along with a myriad of other variables. And in grace and mercy, He considers all of this in His choosing of what tool is best and when it is best to be used. He also knows just how much to use it (or not) as to produce the needed changes for maximum spiritual development and ultimately, fruit growth in mine and others' lives as well. For example: if the soil of my soul is wet with grief, pain, or loss, then application of the fertilizer of compassion and grace can be readily absorbed to prepare my life for the later plowing, planting, and cultivation of spiritual fruit. But if plowing, planting, or cultivation is done when the soil is wet and thus vulnerable, then potentially permanent damage and further soil loss can occur. In contrast, if the soil of my soul is compacted and hardened from repeated sin, then a deep and sustained plowing of relentless conviction might be the best choice to prepare the seedbed for a new planting of the seeds of return, restoration, and renewal. Our Good God is a gentle, wise, and tender gardener who knows and does what is best for this season's crop and those yet to come.

That fact that the Holy Spirit is alive and actively working in me leaves this soil scientist breathless in wonder. It also urges me to discover more about my God in His books of Scripture and nature. Hence, the asking of question after question – not in arrogance or disappointment, but in awe and delight. Neither Scripture nor nature can definitively answer many of the questions posed in this book. Yet I've found that the practice of asking questions and the work of seeking answers alongside the use of spiritual disciplines draws me closer to my Christ. And drawing closer is exactly what I'm hoping for you today! I pray these questions used in conjunction with Scripture and the tools of the spiritual disciplines would be a straight path into joy from a greater intimacy with our Creator God, Who always remembers that we are dust (see Psalm 103:14).

When good caretakers see young ones in their care inching towards exploring something hurtful, they, like God did with Adam in the garden, might ask *"where are you?"* (see Genesis 3:9). The caretakers clearly see and know that little one's desire and drive to explore what could hurt her. Yet the caretakers want to give the little one a chance to practice obedience and trust. Thus, they often ask this question to realign attention and direction in an opportunity for the little one to make the right choice. I can remember my mother doing this often with me, knowing full well where

I was and what trouble I was preparing to explore. She gave me the choice for obedience, just like God did with Adam and Eve, and does every day with us.

God asked questions of Adam and Eve in Eden, Abraham at Sodom and Gomorrah, Moses on Mt. Sinai, and others in the Old Testament. Jesus questioned Nicodemus at night, the rich young ruler in quietness, Saul on the Damascus Road, and the Samaritan woman at the well in the New Testament. Many times, the Holy Spirit does the same with me today when I'm inching (or marching) towards something less than best or harmful to not only me but others. The harmful could be in results or repercussions of shame, guilt, or regret from choices that could even be good, but not best.[4] He often asks, *"where are you?"*. He's God, so of course, He knows exactly where I am and what I'm doing (far better than I do). Yet He gives me opportunity to stop, think, evaluate, and choose the next step (before the next step eats me and my soul alive in disappointment or regret).

However, too many times, I ignore His question because I've stopped listening for His voice speaking from Scripture, saints, situations, or the soil under my feet.[5] And there in my soundproof shell of sin, the rocks are crying out around me because I've stopped worshipping the One Who created them and me (see Luke 19:40). Yet He doesn't stop asking even if I've stopped listening – this book (and others) are tangible evidence of His relentless and beautiful mercy poured out on this soil scientist - hallelujah!

Thus, this question, *"where are you?"* will be repeated in each chapter of this book as we press in to know our Good God more through studying Scripture, nature, and the spiritual disciplines. He knows us fully and longs for us to press in to know Him more. He welcomes our questions and gives wisdom and direction, if we are willing to stop, listen, and consider the answers we find. As importantly, He gives us opportunity to unearth joy from asking questions and subsequent obedience resulting from the new answers discovered in the journey. And those questions I can't answer now can be especially ripe with joy and hope as I discover more and more of my Jesus in the seeking and the asking. For my Jesus is the Answer of Yes and Amen to all of God's many promises (see 2 Corinthians 1:20).

So as one of my former soil science professors used to say at the start of a field trip, "let's go and learn together today". Our glorious Creator God and His wondrous books of Scripture and nature wait for us to dig deeper into their beauty and find fresh hope, courage, joy, and faith to strengthen us for today's demands and the unknowns of the not-yet days to come.

"And those who know your name put their trust in you,
for you, O LORD, have not forsaken those who seek you."
Psalm 9:10 ESV

*This observation isn't meant to separate the Triune God by importance or presence, but rather to emphasize the fullness of all three Persons working together in all ways for the redemption and renewal of souls for all eternity in one amazing love.

[1]Smith, James K.A., in *Practices of Love: Spiritual Disciplines for the Life of the World*, K.D. Bennett, 2017, Brazos Press, Baker Publishing Group, Grand Rapids, MI, p.xii.

[2]deRichter, Daniel B. and Dan H. Yaalon. 2012. "'The Changing Model of Soil' Revisited". Soil Science Society of America Journal, 76:766-778. May, 2012. SSSAJ, Madison, WI.

[3]Disking is a farming practice done to the soil after plowing to further prepare a field for planting, if the soil is especially dense, clumpy, or resistant to forming a good seedbed.

[4]Chambers, O. *My Utmost for His Highest.* In reference to his quote of "the good is the enemy of the best"

[5]soil – I chose that word for multiple reasons – (1) in reference to how God can speak to us through His creation (see Romans 1:18-20 as one example of this idea); (2) soil = a most favorite part of creation for this soil scientist; and (3) it keeps with the alliteration series in that sentence also dearly loved by this soil scientist (haha!).

CULTIVATING
CONSECRATION

I will give you hidden treasures, riches stored in secret places, so
that you may know that I am the LORD, the God of Israel, who
summons you by name.
Isaiah 45:3 NIV

"God has made you and He has assigned you a portion."
E. Elliot[1]

Do you know what your name means? That is, the
meaning of the name given to you by your parent(s).
Mine is Elisabeth, which means consecrated to God. Set
apart. Separated from all else. Indicating a higher purpose or
calling. Thus, the meaning of my name is more than a vo-

1

cation, goal, or characteristic. My name's meaning is itself a trajectory and a telos, both a destination and a desire. Thus, whenever I hear my name, I am reminded of Whom my ultimate telos or sole purpose in life should be, that of Christ Jesus Himself. For Jesus had our Good God's will as his telos and trajectory all the way to the Cross for our salvation. Nothing was too great and no one too small to be included in His purpose for eternity for us (see John 3:16).

I've been called by many other names in my life, some delightful and others not. Yet all these names indicate a relationship or responsibility such as sweetheart or mama, professor or librarian. And when I think about it, a relationship or responsibility can be both a trajectory and a telos in life when considering that today is one piece of eternity as a Christian following hard after God (see Psalm 42:1).

My name meaning *consecrated to God* could also be both a trajectory and a telos because the work of consecration has already been accomplished for me by Christ. I had nothing to do with the choice of my name, much less the true meaning of it. My parents chose this name for me with special attention given to its meaning and its legacy as a family name. Yet the deeper meaning of "set apart" in my life reaches far past even their best intentions.

Jeremiah 1:5 ESV captures this idea. *"Before I formed you in the womb I knew you; and before you were born I consecrated you; I appointed you a prophet to the nations."* This verse resonated deeply with me as a teenager seeking direction and now as a middle-aged woman seeking more than just surviving today. My Good God has the days planned for me in His rightful position as Sovereign (see Psalm 139:16). Yet He gives me the freedom in them to pursue Him in righteousness (see Matthew 6:33) or live as a slave to sin (see Romans 6:1-3).

His plan for my life is simultaneously purposeful, puzzling, and peaceful. He knows the now and the not-yet and keeps all of this in His Hands where He keeps me (see Isaiah 49:16). He has the trajectory of His glory and the good of His people held fast while He Himself is the telos. He holds all things together (including me) while He calls me by name in a voice that I don't always hear, much less listen closely for (see Colossians 1:17 and 1 Kings 19:12).

And He calls me *by name* in this freedom of obedience as seen in Psalm 119:35 GNV: *Direct me in the path of thy commandments, for therein is my delight.* He doesn't just call the roll of names until He gets to the right one (like my husband and I used to do with our sons' names). He calls me as He sees me – consecrated, set apart, chosen, beloved. Not just a meaning of a name, but *by* name as seen in Psalm 139: 1 ESV: *You have searched me and You know me.* For He calls me with incomprehensible purpose, unfathomable grace, and unimaginable love. And He does the very same with you, no matter what name your parent(s) chose for you or what name(s) others choose to call you today, be they admirable, absent, or angry.

Even more incredibly, He does the same every single day with every single one of us eight billion people on earth today; just like He first did with Adam and with every person since him. The fullness of this truth makes me wonder some of my first Eden What-If Questions - Did Adam know the meaning of his name as "reddish" or "like the earth"?[2] Did he realize that the meaning of his name pointed to a trajectory or telos as a caretaker of the earth? Made from soil to care for soil (see Genesis 2:7). Named like soil as to be associated with soil. Quite literally, Adam can be translated as "mud-man."[3] For this soil scientist, that word-picture takes my breath in its beauty and boldness.

Just as beautifully, our Good God remembers today that we are made from dust like He did with Adam those many days ago (see Psalm 103:14 and Genesis 2:7). (And if you're anything like me today, you needed to hear that – He remembers you are dust. Maybe you even need to read that again out loud. For no matter how you are feeling, including as if your soul is being slowly blown away by the dust bowl winds of life-circumstances, our Good God sees you and remembers you as you are and exactly where you are, at this very moment.)

Adam's telos was worshipful obedience of Creator God. Adam's caretaking was the trajectory which would bring him to the bigger picture of worship of Creator God. For in the caretaking of creation, Adam could begin to find this telos of worshipful obedience in caring for the soil from which he was made and instructed to tend.

But there in Eden, Adam probably didn't have to consider the ramifications of soil erosion, salinization, desertification, or soil fertility. He probably knew nothing of humus percentages, cation exchange capacity, microbial biodiversity, or any modern touchpoint for soil health. Yet after Eden, I think Adam knew very well the true gift of the *hidden treasures* found in a healthy soil, since he didn't have them anymore like he did in the Garden (see Genesis 3:17). For the ground was now cursed because of him. In turn, his life and his calling as a caretaker was cursed because of the now-cursed soil under his feet and in his soul.

And this thought makes me wonder – after Eden, did Adam view his own name as a curse or as a reminder of what was now gone? That *adamah*, that "fertile earth" in Eden was only one syllable away from his name but now was forever lost to him. Commentators say that Adam's name could be a play on words in recognition of the *adamah* from which he was made.[2] Adam was a most fitting name in Eden. But after Eden, could Adam's name have become a hard reminder of what was and could still have been, if not for his sin?

Adam's name now meant an intimacy forever lost with the Creator God Who formed him from the dust because of the un-crossable separation of his own sin. (Hang on to that thought about un-crossable, dear reader; the oh-so-good news of the Cross is coming!)

5

And this thought prompts another question - could Adam have realized the deliberate care taken by God for him and all parts of his life sometime during or after he named the animals (see Genesis 2:20)? And that this care even extended to the choice of name of "Adam" for him? With all humility and respect while knowing that nothing or no one is ever overlooked or ignored by our Good God, I dare ask, wouldn't God's deliberate care and attention for Adam also include a special name choice for him?

And I dare ask questions about my own life which might be applicable to your life as well. The first question being, am I actively setting apart my days unto Christ? If you answered anything other than a resounding Yes, then you're in the right place! Please join me on a journey of setting apart the days Christ has set for us, through a trajectory of the spiritual disciplines taking us to the telos of worshipping Him with all our heart, soul, mind and strength. We will ask many questions in this book, about Adam and Eden and us. And hopefully all of these questions will point us straight to Jesus, no matter where our lives might be right now.

As a biologist, I posit Adam might have set up a classification scheme as a good way to accomplish naming the animals. Such a classification scheme might have named the animals based on: how they looked (elephants, giraffes, zebras?), what they did (lions, turtles, groundhogs?), how they smelled (skunks, wildebeest, hogs?), what they ate (anteaters, vultures, bears?), where they lived (coyotes, squirrels, worms?), what sounds they made (owls, wolves, deer?), or by any such characteristics he could identify with his senses. Everything received a name based on at least one of the chosen characteristics in response to at least one or more questions or question sets as expected with a classification scheme. Adam classified creation long before Aristotle, Linnaeus, Darwin, or anyone else attempted to put everything in its place with a name attached to it.

On that train of thought, if Adam named the animals based on a taxonomy of questions, could he then have considered the appropriateness of his own name, "Adam"? Knowing he was formed from adamah ("fertile earth") and given the task to care for the earth, then his name would've been a most logical choice reflecting both his origin from soil and his obligation as caretaker of it. And while we're asking questions, could his name, "Adam", have also been based on his own physical characteristics or abilities similar to Esau ("red" and "hairy") who was so named by his parents in Genesis 25:25? Or could it be something else altogether?

Likewise, could Adam have seen himself as set apart from the animals since he didn't find *a well-matched helper* until God made Eve from his rib (see Genesis 2:18–22 TLV)? Could his name also be a reference to being set apart from those he was tasked to classify and care for? If so, could the name "Adam" have inferred being set apart or consecrated.

Scripture implies that God set Adam apart from the animals, not just in anatomy and physiology but in awareness and purpose. He was set apart with autonomy in choice and assignment in classifying and caretaking.

Genesis 1:31 does tell us that God set apart Adam as being *very good*, in contrast with the rest of creation being considered *good*.

Adam didn't do anything to earn this description; God gave it. Similarly, the ideas about being set apart could apply to us in our designation as Christians, independent of what our given names mean. God set us apart unto Himself through the gift of salvation by Christ's death on the cross for us (see John 3:16). He did for us what we could never do on our own. He gave us new life and new names as His very own, His redeemed. Jesus crossed the un-crossable divide of our sin for us at the Cross – thanks be to God! Jesus did this *once for all* (Romans 6:10 ESV).

And thus, we are set apart to the eternal life that began the day we chose to wear His name as our own. Each of us, all of us set apart to live this day for His Name to be made known. And to do the same again the next day and the day after and…

Thus, as Christ-followers, we are called to worship, whether we study anatomy and physiology or work diligently for awareness and purpose in justice and culture. We are called to worship in our choices as autonomous people and as committed church-goers. We are called to worship in consecrating our days by consistently seeking first the kingdom of heaven in our choices -- according to Matthew 6:33 -- and caretaking for the commitments necessary to our calling of loving God and living in humility, justice, and mercy, found in Micah 6:8.

I've learned that if I'm going to consistently strive to make kingdom choices, I have to always be asking my Good God "What is Your plan?" and listening closely for His answers. (And many times, I can't hear Him if I'm busy making yet another to-do list full of my own ambitions and aspirations.) For if I'm going to be willing to accept His plans, I must acknowledge that this day is His, not mine. Just like every day has been since He set apart the day from the night in Genesis 1.

Whatever the answers may be, questions like this and like my Eden What-If questions can lead us to a new relationship with the Creator God Who formed both Adam and us with love, purpose, and intention for good. For if we are asking questions, we are seeking answers and will find Jesus. And only Jesus is the Yes and Amen for today and eternity (see 2 Corinthians 1:20). For Jesus was the Second Adam Who chose the Cross to bridge sin's un-crossable separation to bind us back together with our Good God (see 1 Corinthians 15:22).

Yet do I actively choose to set apart my days as unto the telos of worship? Do I see the trajectory of obedience drawing me to Christ in worship in those minutes quickly ticking away into another 24-hours? Do I fill my planner with the immediate of meeting the demands of my arrogance or the importance of delivering eternity to others?

Therefore, if anyone cleanses himself from what is dishonorable, he will be a vessel for honorable use, set apart as holy, useful to the master of the house, ready for every good work.
2 Timothy 2:21 ESV

Cultivating Consecration

Just as the farmer waits for rain while he or she works and prays fervently and incessantly, cultivating a new life with new habits formed by new choices requires the same choices of work, time, trust, attention, and prayer. We yearn to return to what was before that year, month, or week lost forever to sin. All the while, we're dreaming of what we've never known before in intimacy with our Creator and the beauty of His creation laid out all around us. The work, the science, and the art of cultivation all mesh into a careful tending of the resources given while looking forward to an outcome beyond the familiar.

Cultivation requires a careful attention as to preparing the soil of a garden or farm for crop growth in removing the weeds, insects, or disease without damaging the tender crop plants themselves. Similarly, cultivating the soil of our souls requires removal of those time and attention eaters which can drain our souls of the refreshing of the Presence of our Creator God. For if we're too busy or distracted with the noise of the now, we can't hear Him. Much less hear Him softly walking in Eden and calling out to us "where are you?" to remind us exactly of where we are – lost in the choking grip of worry, envy, greed, arrogance, denial, or apathy which have hardened the soil of our souls even without our realization.

Can you picture with me the prodigal son's father always watching the road for his son? Perched on the edge of his seat, eyes shaded by his hand in the hopes of seeing just a little further around that corner? Ready to leap up at a moment's notice to tuck his robe into his belt and run with all his strength down the road with hands lifted and waving while calling his son's name? Abandoned with joy, alive with hope – nothing is as important as that son which once was lost but now is found. If you can picture that, then you have a taste of what our Creator God is doing now as He awaits you to stop, think, turn, and come back with the first step towards cultivating consecration.

Take some time to look up, write out, and meditate on each of the Scriptures in this chapter, presented in order of appearance.

1. Isaiah 45:3
2. John 3:16
3. Psalm 4:21
4. Jeremiah 1:5
5. Psalm 139:16
6. Matthew 6:33
7. Romans 6:1-3
8. Isaiah 49:16
9. Colossians 1:17
10. 1 Kings 19:12
11. Psalm 119:35
12. Psalm 139:1
13. Genesis 2:7
14. Psalm 103:14
15. Genesis 3:17, 5:2, 3:20, 2:20, 25:25, 2:18-22, and 1:3
16. Romans 6:10
17. Romans 3:23
18. Micah 6:8
19. 2 Corinthians 1:20
20. 1 Corinthians 15:22
21. 2 Timothy 2:21

Questions to consider:

Which of these verses nourished the soil of your soul today with hope, joy, courage, or faith?

Did any of these verses remind you of other Scripture passages or stories which made you stop and think about the status of the soil of your soul? If so, then list the other passages or stories and their importance to your life today.

Which of these verses (the ones in this chapter or ones you were reminded of) could be helpful to someone else in your life today? Take some time to send a verse or two to a friend in a text, email, note, or card. Not only will the other person be helped by this act, so will you, as the writing of the verse(s) will again reinforce truth and right thinking in your mind and the soil of your soul.

Which of these verses do you need to write on a card or to-do list to come back to again tomorrow (and days again afterwards) for more reflection, prayer, and reframing of your perspective as to align your heart with His?

Exercises to do:

1. Take a walk outside in a natural or wooded area, farm or greenspace, if possible. If not, then set aside some time for a YouTube or Bing images tour of nature in a natural area near your home. While you're walking (be it literally or virtually), take a quick count of some of the different types of plants,

animals, mushrooms, insects, rocks, and soils around you. If you were Adam and had been given the role of classifier of creation, how would you have delineated these different organisms into groupings or orders? What questions would you have asked or pondered while assigning names to them? Think creatively to use the tools and senses you already have (or can look up), as well as other identifying features – such as sight, hearing, smell, touch, location, or habits of the organism. Write a few of your questions or classification designations here. Take special note of this place and time to associate the memory with the choice to set aside time for worship during your day, as an act of consecrating it and yourself to our Good God.

2. Take some time to thank God for some of the specific and beautiful things and their differences which you saw on your walk. Then, take some time to look at yourself in a mirror and thank God for how He has made you with purpose and specificity in beauty different from all others. Thank Him for how He has consecrated you for now. He has set this time, this place, and this task before you, even if you might feel otherwise. Our Good God has a purpose and a plan for you in all moments of all days. Nothing is wasted with Him. Return to this exercise if you struggle with

bringing up gratitude from the soil of your soul. He will hear and He will soften your soul, if you persist in bringing an offering of thanksgiving. He awaits your sacrifice of staying until your heart is full and your gratitude is genuine.

3. If a certain friend or family member has come to your mind during these exercises, take some time to pray for him or her to discover the specific beauty God has placed in his or her life. Consider making this person a regular part of your prayer time for the next six days, that he or she might know that they are dearly loved and considered as very good by our Creator God.

"Where are you?" (Genesis 3:9b) questions for this chapter:

Has your definition or opinion of being consecrated unto God as a Christian changed in any way since starting this chapter? If so, how?

Rank how you perceive your life as being consecrated to God (or not) with 1 being "I'm number one and I like it that way, thank you very much" to 10 being "my life is not my own but Christ's". Write your answer and today's date here _____.

Look up Galatians 2:20 in at least three different Bible versions than the one you normally use (biblegateway.com and YouVersion are two great resources for doing this step easily). Now write out this verse in the version which spoke the most to you.

Pray this verse aloud after you've finished writing it. Re-read the verse again. Plan on returning to repeat the prayer and re-reading the steps again at least once later today.

Now looking back over this chapter, has anything come to mind that could be helping your choice in consecration or hindering it? If so, write it here.

Reflection prayer:

Dear Father God,

Thank You that You don't change, even when my circumstances and feelings about them do. Thank You that You call me to be Yours completely in Your magnificent love. Thank You that You provided a way for me to return to You in Jesus' death, burial, and resurrection. Thank You for the amazing forgiveness You give me every single day. Please help me in the journey of consecrating all parts of my life as Yours. Please help me to learn faithfulness in making both big and seemingly small choices for righteousness to fill my life.

In the strong Name of Jesus,

Amen.

*These questions spur myriads more, such as who taught Adam how to speak, what to say, and the meanings for the words? Babies learn from parents, siblings, teachers, and others – who did Adam learn from? Or did he create language himself and taught it to Eve? And then on to Cain and Abel? Those questions could easily be the start of another book, or a blog series. Talk about food for thought for this soil scientist...

[1]Elliot, Elisabeth. As taken from her lecture, "Giving Your Life Away, Part 1", YouTube, as posted by the Elisabeth Elliot Foundation on Instagram, 6/29/22.

[2]Davis, Ellen. 2014. Scripture, Culture, and Agriculture: An Agrarian Reading of the Bible. Cambridge University Press, New York, p. 29.

[3]Personal communication, Dr. Kelvin Moore, Hebrew scholar, School of Theology and Missions, Union University, 9/9/21.

CULTIVATING
CONFESSION

*For godly grief produces a repentance that leads to salvation
without regret, whereas worldly grief produces death.*
2 Corinthians 7:10 ESV

This God is my strong refuge and has made my way blameless.
2 Samuel 22:33 ESV

This God—his way is perfect; the word of the LORD *proves
true; he is a shield for all those who take refuge in him.*
Psalm 18:30 ESV

*"The Christian life is about bringing all things under Christ
and allowing the Spirit to convict us and guide us in everyday,
mundane activities. The Spirit does this through spiritual
disciplines that influence and impact those around us."*
K.D. Bennett[1]

Well Grounded

Could the "Okies from Muskogee" who left the Midwest during the Dust Bowl for a new life in California or Oregon have felt like Adam after Eden? John Steinbeck in his book, *Grapes of Wrath,* wrote of their loss and how they faced it with bravery and perseverance. Those Dust Bowl refugees were survivors of tragedy and seekers of triumph. We can see that same bravery and perseverance lived out today by refugees fleeing war-torn and sin-ravaged homelands. They're fleeing not just for their own lives, but for the lives of their children and their children's children not yet born. They are trading their next breath for the soil on which they were born.

Could (or do) refugees have known defeat or despair, longing and loss, and uncertainty with unanswered questions? Adam's sin forced him from Eden. Dust Bowl refugees fled once-Eden-like productive Midwestern farmlands. Modern-day refugees often escape their hells with nothing more than the clothes on their backs. All regret choices made, either of their own making or of others in power over them. All mourn what once-was and now-isn't. All yearn for return to what would never be for their lifetimes while hoping for liberty and life for their children and children's children. All grieve what should-have-been while trying to survive another 24-hours of what never-should-have-been.

I wonder, could David have felt something similar as he fled again and again from his pursuers who wanted nothing less than his life? Psalm 5:11ESV *But let all who take refuge in you rejoice; let them ever sing for joy, and spread your protection over them, that those who love your name may exult in you* and Psalm 7:1ESV *O LORD my God, in you do I take refuge; save me from all my pursuers and deliver me* could suggest he did. More importantly, these verses and many others give us a glimpse into David's faith. His faith remained solid even when he was on the outside looking into a kingdom which was supposed to have been his (see 1 Samuel 16:1-13).

Even if Adam couldn't have physically looked back into Eden, he could have seen it in the dust on his body and replayed it in his memories every day afterwards. Dust Bowl refugees literally saw their once fertile soil borne aloft as dust by the wind, out of their reach and out of their lives all along their way West. Modern-day refugees might see their homes or lands through a haze of tears and a grid of barbed wire, armored tanks, and angry men. Whether seen by the eye or the eye of the mind, pictures of homes and hopes lost are vivid and lasting in their impact on the lives of all involved, including those of us watching the news or reading the Scriptures.

Adam had fiery and fearsome angels preventing his return to Eden (see Genesis 3:24), while current refugees are held back by soldiers brandishing AK-47's and bullet bandoliers. Thousands of acres of bare soil devoid of hope achieved the same effect of fear for the Dust Bowl refugees. Even though David had an army of mighty men, he knew it was not enough for the much bigger and stronger enemy armies, including those enemies of sin (see 2 Samuel 11). All knew what they'd lost. All knew they couldn't regain it. Thus, they bore deep scars of loss that would impact their lives from that day onwards.

Thoughts like these prompt me to ask the following questions: Could the soil of Adam's soul have been permanently eroded by his sin and thus been left there in Eden without him? Could the Dust Bowl have ravaged the soil of the Okies' souls like it did the soil formerly under their feet? Could terrorists or tyrants have torched the gardens of the modern-day refugees' hearts like they did to their homes, schools, and churches? Could sin's furrows etched deep in David's soul and Israel's history have reoriented his children's trajectory towards sin instead of Sovereign God?

When I emerged scarred, empty, and numb after two and a half years of life-changing sin-choices in college, others commented that I was a different person than before. And I was. I had been metamorphosed in thinking, goals, habits, friends, and priorities. Almost the only thing that remained the same was my name and hair color. Even when I heard my name spoken after that time running away from God, it almost seemed foreign or ill-fitting.

These thoughts bring to mind the following questions: could Adam have wanted to change his name after Eden to reflect the immensity of a life forever changed by sin? Like Naomi did in changing her name to Mara ("bitter") after the death of her husband and sons in her despair and grief (see Ruth 1:20)? Like many refugees do when they enter a new life in a new country or city? A new name could provide protection from many threats, ranging from choking grief and anxiety to evil people still hunting those refugees. A new name could give a new mindset of hope in a seemingly tenuous freedom. A new name could begin a needed change in mindset from refugee to a life restored.

Or could Adam have longed for God to have changed his name for him? Like God did with Abram to Abraham as to indicate a new promise and a fresh beginning with hope (see Genesis 17:5 respectively)? Adam was the one who sinned, but God was always the One Who had a plan for him, knowing the payment required for his sin. And God's forever plan for Adam and all of us was the birth, life, death, burial, and resurrection of the One named Jesus (see Revelation 4:8). Jesus, the second Adam and the One to Whose Name all bow, is the only One Who could rename death as defeated and the grave as gone (see Romans 5:14 and Philippians 2:10). Jesus, our Emmanuel, the One Who gave us new names and positions as sons and daughters forever (see Galatians 3:26).

Even with a name change, someone still can think of himself as he was before it. For if the person still sees himself as he did before a name change, he defines himself by his name and what it meant to him. Thus, it doesn't matter what his name is now. For to him, he will always be what he sees himself as – victim or victor, refugee or restorer, tenuous or tenacious, and such. Thus, after Eden, did Adam still see himself as the Adam hiding his nakedness in shame and fear even if the *adamah* under his feet was different? Scripture doesn't answer this question, but it can shed a lot of light on my own life today.

How do I see myself today? Do I see myself as I truly am? If so, then I should be seeing myself as rescued and redeemed, with my name written in the Lamb's book of life forever (see Revelation 21:27). But does my life reflect this truth? Does my life show my new identity and my new name as Christ's own? Or if not, what does my life show?

Which of the following would best describe me today? Christ-follower or curious bystander, trusting or tentative, faithful or fearful, obedient or opportunistic, content or consumer, grateful or grabbing? Oh, how I wish that I could always say the first of each of those contrasts describes my life! For I know that the first contrasts characterize how I should be living, having been given the name of beloved, chosen child of God. Yet all too many times, the second contrasts of my old name and identity before Christ are most evident in how I am choosing to live my life. All too often, I am here trying to live life from a soul eroded by sin, ignoring my Redeemer. He waits to restore me yet again with the strong grace and mercy unearthed in the spiritual discipline of repentance.

David knew this principle of repentance, restoration, and renewal. And he embraced it – may I do the same as he did in Psalm 51! On that note, please stop for a while to read, sit, and soak in the power of his words in that hard and beautiful chapter. And after you've sat here a while with Psalm 51 to let it penetrate the soil of your soul, then it will be time to go on in the good work of repentance. Then, go on to Psalm 23 and sit there for a while so it can soak in and strengthen you for that work. For repentance demands the difficult work of fleeing sin as a refugee into mercy and grace which joins us to our God and our Jesus, Who is always our Refuge and Redeemer (see Psalm 62:8 and 78:35).

2 Corinthians 7:10 captures the placement, purpose, and position for repentance when I admit that I have sinned and am a refugee in need of much mercy and grace with the following words: *For godly grief produces a repentance that leads to salvation without regret, whereas worldly grief produces death.* Only God can take the grief of loss, pain, and rejection and transform it into good (see Romans 8:28).

Thus, as a Christ-follower and soil scientist, I see a most lovely cycle of life in the choice of repentance. Remorse leads to repentance. Repentance to return. Return to restoration. Restoration to renewal. Renewal to joining another in his or her repentance.

And the cycle continues outward like ripples in a pond from a single stone. This cycle is regenerative. For when I confess my sin, I am opened to join another in compassion, consolation, and commitment, which leads to confession. And there in confession, my arrogance is quieted so I can hear another's need to be made new by the love found at the Cross. For only there at the Cross can repentance begin.

When I choose to join another in repentance, I can help him enter this cycle of confession and commitment. And in the cycle, he can become re-created in the soil of his soul. And onward and outward goes this cycle, from one to another and often, back again. Each iteration of the cycle plows deeper into my heart for removing a tendency for sin, and further out into others' hearts for the same.

We see this idea played out in many cycles in the natural world around us, a true cycle of breathing fresh life into the once-dead dust of the soil of our souls. New life brings more death that leads to more life and so on. Only the cycle of confession can unearth the *adamah* of a soul once alive like Adam was in Eden. Only the cycle of confession can bring new life to a dusty soul buried in the fall-out and waste of sin's lies.

The Holy Spirit began this cycle of confession in my life when He first convicted me of my sin as a child. And thanks be to God, He is faithful to keep convicting as I sin now. For every time I am obedient and confess in repentance, I am re-created and made ready to join another in compassion with her loss to sin. And when she is restored and renewed, she is readied for joining with another in need of repentance's renewal. Only God can do such a good work in one life, much less in many lives. Yet this good work can change a world forever– may it be so with us, Jesus!

For when I repent, God not only frees me from my sin but fills my soul with the treasures of mercy, grace, faith, and hope. I wonder if these treasures He gives to me in repentance could be compared to how the Israelites escaped Egypt with the plunder of their captors (see Exodus 12:36)? The Israelites trusted in obedience, and God gave them what they never would have received otherwise, much less earned. Their treasures didn't wear out, fade, or rust in 40-years of desert wanderings, but were used as crown jewels in the tabernacle and temple (see Exodus 26 and 1 Kings 6). Similarly, my treasures of this grace, mercy, faith, and hope do not fade, decay, or rust. Rather, they grow in and out of my life into others' lives as prompts for their repentance, re-creation, and receiving of these treasures too (see Matthew 6:19). And together, our treasures become the crown jewels in our lives that mark us as Christ's and draw others who are wandering without purpose or hope to find a new life forever in Christ too.

Hosea 6:1 ESV expresses the unmistakable and lasting beauty of repentance: *Come, let us return to the* LORD; *for he has torn us, that he may heal us; he has struck us down, and he will bind us up.* How many times have I read that verse, Psalm 51, or others through a veil of tears, awash in the grief and loss of the sin I have (yet again) let furrow deep in the soil of my soul? More times than I can count, unfortunately. But I can count how many times my Good God hasn't welcomed me back with mercy and grace – ZERO! Every single time I came, He was already there.

Waiting for me to return, like other prodigals before me have done (see Luke 15:11-32).

No matter how long I ran or what I did in the running, He was there.

Just like He was there for me this morning when I ran back yet again to Him.

Just like He is here for you now. Can you hear Him calling your name?

If we confess our sins, he is faithful and just to forgive us our sins and to cleanse us from all unrighteousness.
1 John 1:9 ESV

Cultivating Confession

Confession is not the most enjoyable activity, but it is the most necessary. For when I confess, then I am cleansed. When I am cleansed, I am restored to wholeness. And nothing compares to the freedom and joy of wholeness. For in wholeness, I am fully present with God and He with me. Thus, when I see confession as a necessary step to wholeness, then confession can change me into the child which comes easily, simply, and naturally to Jesus. And the child who stays there with Him (see Matthew 19:14).

Take some time to look up, write out, and meditate

on each of the Scriptures in this chapter, presented in order of appearance.

1. 2 Corinthians 7:10
2. 2 Samuel 22:33
3. Psalm 18:30
4. Psalm 5:11
5. Psalm 7:1
6. 1 Samuel 16:1-13
7. Genesis 3:24
8. 2 Samuel 11
9. Ruth 1:20
10. Genesis 17:5
11. Revelation 4:8
12. Romans 5:14
13. Philippians 2:10
14. Galatians 3:26
15. Revelation 21:27
16. Psalm 51
17. Psalm 23
18. Psalm 62:8
19. Psalm 78:35
20. Romans 8:28
21. Exodus 12:36
22. Exodus 26 and 1 Kings 6
23. Matthew 6:19
24. Hosea 6:1
25. Luke 15:11-32

26. 1 John 1:9
27. Matthew 19:14

Questions to consider:

Which of these verses nourished the soil of your soul today with hope, joy, courage, or faith?

Did any of these verses remind you of other Scripture passages or stories which made you stop and think about the status of the soil of your soul? If so, then list the other passages or stories and their importance to your life today.

Which of these verses (the ones in this chapter or ones you were reminded of) could be helpful to someone else in your life today? Take some time to send a verse or two to a friend in a text, email, note, or card. Not only will the other person be helped by this act, so will you as the writing of the verse(s) will again reinforce truth and right thinking in your mind and the soil of your soul.

Which of these verses do you need to write on a card or to-do list to come back to again tomorrow (and days again afterwards) for more reflection, prayer, and reframing of your perspective as to align your heart with His?

Exercises to do:

1. Disclaimer: this is probably something different (but if you've known me before now, that's probably what you expect) – but have you considered using the time spent deep-cleaning your bathroom, kitchen, garage, or any area that might need some extra elbow-grease and attention (without too much mental focus) as a time of confession? To call out those pesky grimy sins as you scrub those soaked-in stains. To list those pervasively stubborn sin-habits as you're working to remove the physical dirt in front of you. To let your tears of repentance mix with the water, soap, or bleach on the wet tub, sink, shelf, or floor receiving the work of your hands. To use this time to pray for the cleansing of the soil of your soul in areas that are painful or hard to reach as you do the same with the corners, edges, or areas hidden or forgotten in the rush of everyday chores. And then, when you've finished the physical cleaning with your hands, this bathroom, kitchen, garage, or such can be a tangible reminder of the eternal good work of confession that you've done before our Good God. Likewise, the clean freedom of confession in your soul can energize you with the very good work He did in your soul with forgiveness and restoration when you asked. (Similarly, the

need to return in the future to clean whatever you just finished working on will be a reminder for your need to return again in confession and repentance, if it's been a while...)

2. Another opportunity for confession and restoration can always be found in the garden, farm, or flower-pot. First the weeding, digging or hoeing up, and then the removal of weeds, stubble, or blown-in trash can bring a satisfaction of the good work that it is. The pulling up and out of that sin or temptation is always refreshing in the looking towards a life without it – similar to a repotting or transplanting of a plant stunted or choked from lack of room, be it from a too-small pot or weed pressure. Take some time to clean out the soil of your soul while working with your hands in the soil underneath your feet or next to you in a pot. Then afterwards, while washing your hands with soap and water to remove the dirt, thank God for His good gifts of mercy, grace, and forgiveness that have already washed away the sin from your soul which you confessed earlier. Pray that the water spilling over your hands be as mercy spilling out of your life into others in compassion, grace, mercy, and love. And let your clean hands and the good smell of soap be a reminder to pray for family, friends, coworkers,

neighbors, and church members in their need for confession and repentance.

3. Finally, look up the song, "Change My Heart, Oh God" and listen to it all the way through. If you know it already, sing it aloud (or in your head if you need to be quiet in consideration of others). I often sing this simple song and read Psalm 51 aloud as a time of confession and repentance. For some reason or another, this song with that Scripture seems to invite the Holy Spirit to soften the soil of my soul and allow for confession and repentance of even the most stubborn of sins.

"Where are you?" (Genesis 3:9b) questions for this chapter:

1. If you were to rate the status of your soul now in regards to how long it's been since you've had a time of confession, where would you fall on the scale?

   Remember, this evaluation is just between you and God - be true and reasonable in your ranking.

   Rate the status of your heart with a number from 1 to 10. With 1 being clean, gleaming, white, and clear, and 10 being caked-on dirt, stand-up-on-their-own dirty, smell-before-you-see-them stained pants.

2. What specific sins or less-than-helpful habits come to mind quickly now? List them here in order of most effect on your life and the lives of those in your life.

3. Take some time to ask for the Holy Spirit to soften your heart to know true godly sorrow and the gift of repentance for these sins or habits. Schedule brief intentional times in the next few days to ask Him to keep revealing to you what you might not see now but that needs to be removed from your life for a greater intimacy with Him in the freedom of the clean soil of your soul.

Reflection prayer:

Dear Father God,

Thank You that You are always there waiting for me to return to You. Thank You that You give mercy, grace, and forgiveness again and again. Thank You that You know me fully and love me still. Please harrow my heart and work godly sorrow deep into the soil of my soul, that I might cultivate confession and repentance. Please let my confession be of good to others in their repentance to return to You. Please replace sin's furrows in my life with obedience so that the rains of Your mercies might flow down into my inmost parts and soften the roots of bitterness, callousness, shame, guilt, and regret buried there. Please remove these roots and their seeds and replant my life with Your good seeds of strong grace and righteousness.

In the strong Name of Jesus,

Amen.

[1]Bennett, K.D., 2017. "Practices of Love: Spiritual Disciplines for the Life of the World". Brazos Press, Baker Publishing Group, Grand Rapids, MI. p. 16.

CULTIVATING CONFIDENCE

*And they heard the voice of the L*ORD *God, walking in the garden in the cool of the day: and Adam and his wife hid themselves from the presence of the L*ORD *God amongst the trees of the garden.*
Genesis 3:8 KJV

At one time you were far away from God. But now you belong to Christ Jesus. He spilled his blood for you. This has brought you near to God. Christ himself is our peace. He has made Jews and Gentiles into one group of people. He has destroyed the hatred that was like a wall between us.
Ephesians 2:13-14 NIRV

Remain [Abide] in me, and I will ·remain [abide] in you. A branch cannot produce fruit ·alone [by itself] but must ·

*remain [abide] in the vine. In the same way, you cannot
produce fruit alone but must ·remain [abide] in me.*
John 15:4 EXB

*"God, what is man's best gift to mankind? To be beautiful of
soul and then let people see into your soul."*
R.J. Foster[1]

I*just want to go home.* Have you ever said that with tears
from deep in the soil of your soul?

Maybe you've said that as a prodigal son or daughter.
Maybe you've said that wanting relief from very hard life
situations not of your own making. Maybe you've said that
in the pain, grief, and loss of death or separation from a
beloved one. Maybe you've not allowed yourself to say that
because if you did, the dam holding back the tears would
crumble and so would you.

I can remember not letting myself say that aloud
when I was in the hospital before and after our first son's
high-risk birth. Because of his needs, I had to spend weeks
in a special hospital two hours away from my husband and
eight hours away from my parents. I didn't know anyone
there except Jesus.

But Jesus didn't just come to visit, He stayed during
those long days and longer nights of tests, doctor visits, and

little or no sleep. He spoke peace when the doctors said otherwise. He brought hope when the symptoms got worse. He taught me how to find my home in Him, especially in the last place I wanted to be.

Even though it's been twenty-five years now, I still vividly remember reading and holding fast to this passage over and again – Romans 8:18 JUB: *For I know with certainty that the sufferings of this present time* **are** *not worthy* to be compared *with the coming glory which shall be manifested in us.* So much so, the pages in the Bible I used at that time are wavy and crinkled with runny ink-stains from the tears that dripped upon those repeatedly underlined words. I'd read and cry and read again aloud trying to convince my heart that I would see the glory of this baby boy made manifest in trusting my Good God with what I couldn't do anything about. Long story short – our son is now a man who dearly loves his God and his family of a lovely wife and beautiful little girl who will soon be a big sister!

But not all my stories have happy endings, and that's ok. For I know that no matter what happens, God can be trusted to be my abiding place. He is my home and thus, my confidence in life. And if He's my home and my confidence, I can truly be what He's made me to be, no matter where or with whom I might find myself. And the same can be true for you.

On this idea, I wonder if Adam might've had similar thoughts about wanting to go home to the Garden after the fall and being put out of Eden. He didn't have what I often take for granted every day. He didn't have the benefit of hearing others' stories about how God brought them through hard life circumstances (see Hebrews 12:1). He didn't have the gift of reading Scripture's promises of God as faithful in sustaining, providing, remaining, or protecting (see Psalm chapters 41 and 136). He only had the memories of what he knew in Eden, Eve, and what he could now see around him in the land (see Genesis 3:23-24). Even though my father and I are most "us" in songs, stories, speech, and satisfaction when we are out on the land at our family farm, we don't find assurance or confidence from the land itself. The land merely realigns our thoughts and hearts to our true confidence, our Good God Who made it and us for His purpose and plan.

I posit Adam couldn't find his confidence for today or the not-yet in what he knew or where he lived; it had to come from his God. Scripture doesn't tell us the details of Adam's life, especially his thoughts or words, but it does tell us what to do with our lives, including our thoughts and words (see Colossians 2:6 and 3:17, 2 Thessalonians 2:17, and 1 John 2:27). (On that note, please remember that no person's words can give us the very best instructions for our words, thoughts, or lives. Only Scripture can do that as it comes from our Good God to us and for us to seek and find Him in (see 2 Timothy 3:16-17).)

Adam's inclination in Eden after his sin was to hide (see Genesis 3:8). Did that tendency travel with him after Eden? Again, Scripture doesn't tell us more on this, but isn't hiding what we often see as a natural first (or at least a second) response to an unknown or potentially fearful situation? This response isn't reserved to a specific generation, time, or people; it's found throughout Scripture in Adam's descendants, including Abraham, Jacob, Elijah, David, and Peter just to name a few. We can still see this response in our lives today, in many situations, including typical American church culture.

For example:

- The hiding of our true God-given personalities as to conform with what's expected in our traditions and expectations.
- The hiding of our pain and fears as to easily converse with all the other seemingly shiny, happy people in our churches, Bible studies, or small groups.
- The hiding of our weaknesses as to conceal that "we (don't) got this" in our homes and hopes or jobs or journeys.
- The hiding of our lack of confidence in our God as to convey that all parts of our lives are under His control as Christians.
- The hiding of our strengths as to camouflage the distinctive beauty God has crafted in us for His glory to be displayed.
- The hiding of our idols as to cover our lack of contentment that can't be satisfied by anything or anyone other than our choosing to abide in our God.

(I surely hope you don't struggle with hiding like I do. Please know I'm here to confess, not condemn, all the while praying you might find something here that's encouraging to you.)

We can talk all about masks, hiding, and needing to be honest and open with each other and with ourselves. But it's just blowing hot air if our lives don't reflect our abiding in our Good God as our confidence and our true home by choosing to trust Him with the results of our obedience to Him. Obedience is necessary in both words and choices. I've learned that choices are essential in abiding. Choices like holding hard to the truths of Scripture and stepping forward in faith in speaking the truth in love to another needing hope and encouragement or rebuke and repentance (see Ephesians 4:15, 1 John 3:18, and Proverbs 27:6). Choosing to do what's right and under the Holy Spirit's direction even if it's unfamiliar or uncomfortable (see Joshua 24:15 and Romans 8:14). Being open and honest with others about our lives that aren't as we'd hoped for, dreamed of, or longed for because of pain, grief, or loss while acknowledging a need for more faith (see 2 Corinthians 4:7-11 and Mark 9:24). None of these choices are easy; none of these choices are one-time events. I must keep choosing to cultivate that confidence in my God. I must abide, remain, dwell in Him day in and day out especially when it seems far easier to hide, run, or hold back part of the truth like Adam did (see Genesis 3:9-13).

Those verses I prayed and cried over in the hospital years ago, along with many others since, have shown me that God wants me as I was then and now today – exhausted, helpless, and struggling to believe past the demands of chronic health conditions. Like the song goes, "Just as I am, I come to Thee" – He calls me to come and sit right there with Him and trust that He's gonna take care of every single thing. I couldn't hide my need in the hospital from Him. That lesson helps me understand that I don't need to hide my need from Him or those He's placed in my life today. He's taught me to not try to make things work all on my own in my own way, even if I think it might make me look better (which is really hiding, isn't it?). He's shown me there's much strength to be found in vulnerability. Not just strength for me, but for others. For all of us struggle to make it through something hard sometime along the way. And my Good God takes care of all things for me, even and especially in the details of even one day that are often overwhelming, including today. He gives. I receive. And I think that's the heart of abiding.

For when I am abiding in God as my confidence, I don't have to hide like Adam did. Not that hiding did Adam a lot of good; God knew exactly where he was and what he'd done. And God loved Adam there just as much after he'd sinned as He did before. Just like God does for each and every one of us, He loves us as much today and He did before we did whatever it was we did in fear and lack of faith (see 1 John 3:1 and 4:16). I think Paul knew this kind of confidence in our God very well. He didn't hide; he stood up and proclaimed truth. He did this in making tents or in temples; He did it in prison and the palace. He knew God as his home, his confidence wherever he was. His confidence wasn't in his knowledge, training, or heritage; his confidence was in his God (see Philippians 3:3-6). And we have that same opportunity today as Paul did years ago – to abide in Christ and thus, find our confidence only in our God. We don't have to hide like Adam; we can abide like Paul. On that note, now would be a great time to stop and savor the reading of a chapter or more from Philippians. Be sure and jot a few notes in the margins here or in your Bible of what God brings to your mind in how you can live confidently in light of what you read from Philippians about Paul's life.

Paul lived confidently because he abided in God, day in and day out. For he knew the value and the victory of abiding like John talked about in John chapter 15. He knew Christ as the Vine and him as a branch off the Vine (see John 15:5). The essence of life flowed out from his Christ into his life and equipped him for whatever was there in front of him, whether or not it was familiar, friendly, or foreboding.

Similarly, abiding strengthens my confidence I found in God by recognizing and reminding me that I can't do anything good outside of Christ, while reinforcing that nothing is impossible with Him (see John 15:4 and Luke 1:37). The realizing that I must abide in Christ keeps me staying in hard situations where He's called me to go or to follow Him in moving into the unfamiliar or unknown (see Matthew 16:24). For if I'm abiding in God, then my confidence is found in Him with the truth that He will take anything and everything and use it for good in His plan and purpose (see Romans 8:28). And that promise is true, even if I might not see the good in the now or not-yet (see Hebrews 11:1).

God has made each of us as we are for His glory and the good of His people, just like He did Adam and Paul. I know this truth, but do I live like I believe it when I hide under a false humility that I can't do something? When I hide questions for a decision made by another that lacks wisdom, grace, or discernment? When I hide from needs in others' lives which could be met by resources in my possession or abilities? When I hide my needs from others which could be met by their resources or abilities? And on and on… bottom line: when I'm hiding, I'm not abiding.

I have many opportunities every day to hide from others or abide with God. For me, daily examples are such things as: hiding my needs of physical help for my health conditions by not asking for or receiving volunteered help or by simply saying "I'm fine." Or I can abide in God's plan of acknowledging the need and the grace given by Him to others who truly care and want to help. Hiding my God-given gifts by telling myself (or others) that I'm not qualified for a task because I know of someone else who's far better at it and I'm intimidated by stepping forward. Or

I can abide in God's plan by claiming Ephesians 2:10 GNT as His provision for me in doing the task in His promise of *God has made us what we are, and in our union with Christ Jesus he has created us for a life of good deeds, which he has already prepared for us to do*. I can hide my personality and heart-felt desires by not responding to another's queries because I don't want to feel out-of-place or misunderstood. Or I can abide by simply, humbly saying what's in my heart that honors God and trust Him to take the words and translate them into what will encourage another.

Hiding is my default; abiding is my decision. God calls me to courage in all things (see Joshua 1:9). Bravery is not my default but choosing it is an opportunity to show I'm finding confidence in my Good God (and Him alone). David captured this idea in Psalm 17:8 DARBY: *Keep me as the apple of thy eye, hide me under the shadow of thy wings.* David knew he was deeply loved and tenderly cared for by God, hence the reference to *apple of thy eye*. He also knew his tendency to be afraid and choose disobedience, hence the *hide me under the shadow of thy wings*. And there in the joining of these ideas lies the secret of finding confidence in God – relying on and reveling in His love for me while resting in His providing for me. For if I'm resting, then I'm not out doing something other than abiding.

David did in Psalm 17:8 what I should be doing right now about situations in my life, including finishing the writing of this book. I wonder if Adam and Paul and so many others did the same with their life challenges? I know I did that there in the hospital 25 years ago and I've done it many times since then. I've heard my parents, grandparents, and other mentors do exactly that in a variety of situations. In all of that, God hasn't ever turned away or not provided what is needed when it was needed.

And I'm hoping that you'll do the same today- not to hide but to choose to abide in God as your confidence and true home - in whatever situation or opportunity or person in front of you. That you'll make choices which cultivate your confidence in our Good God. That you'll show your family, neighbors, coworkers, friends, and strangers that you can be brave and be bold and be the you He's made you to be, no matter whether your life seems like a Garden of Eden (or not).

Cultivating confidence

All kinds of people have said all kinds of things about cultivating confidence. And even if it sounds good, their theories aren't anything more than dirt if they're not fully grounded in Scripture and prayer to our Good God. Because, as Christians, only God is our confidence and home. We are no longer *aliens* or *strangers;* we are His own (Ephesians 2:19 ESV). There is no other "home away from home" outside our Good God. For only our Good God can truly be our confidence in all situations for only He goes before us, stands with us, and is our Rear Guard at all times. He is our Rock and Redeemer Who doesn't leave or change or stop in lavishing love. And He's calling us today to come home to Him and find that He is our confidence and our true home as He's said many times in Scripture and will gently remind us in the soil of our souls in prayer.

Take some time to look up, write out, and meditate on each of the Scriptures in this chapter, presented in order of appearance.

1. Genesis 3:8
2. Ephesians 2:13-14
3. John 15:4
4. Romans 8:18
5. Hebrews 12:1
6. Psalm 41 and 136
7. Genesis 3:23-24
8. Colossians 2:6 and 3:17
9. 2 Thessalonians 2:17
10. 1 John 2:27
11. 2 Timothy 3:16-17
12. Genesis 3:8
13. Ephesians 4:15
14. 1 John 3:18
15. Proverbs 27:6
16. Joshua 24:15

17. Romans 8:14
18. 2 Corinthians 4:7-11
19. Mark 9:24
20. Genesis 3:9-13
21. 1 John 3:1 and 4:16
22. Philippians 3:3-6
23. John 15:4-5
24. Luke 1:37
25. Matthew 16:24
26. Romans 8:28
27. Hebrews 11:1
28. Ephesians 2:10
29. Joshua 1:9
30. Psalm 17:8
31. Ephesians 2:19

Questions to consider:

Which of these verses nourished the soil of your soul today with hope, joy, courage, or faith?

Did any of these verses remind you of other Scripture passages or stories which made you stop and think about the status of the soil of your soul? If so, then list the other passages or stories and their importance to your life today.
Which of these verses (the ones in this chapter or ones you were reminded of) could be helpful to someone else in your

life today? Take some time to send a verse or two to a friend in a text, email, note, or card. Not only will the other person be helped by this act, so will you as the writing of the verse(s) will again reinforce truth and right thinking in your mind and the soil of your soul.

Which of these verses do you need to write on a card or to-do list to come back to again tomorrow (and days again afterwards) for more reflection, prayer, and reframing of your perspective as to align your heart with His?

Exercises to do:

1. Draw, in a picture or in words, the place you consider (most) as home to you. Home meaning that place (or time spent at a place) where you are the most "you." Be sure to include people, sounds, smells, tastes, touch, experiences, phrases, emotions, and anything else that comes to mind as "home" for you. Do you see a theme that could in turn describe you as "you" in this picture? If so, write it here: _____

   _____

   _____

   Now take some time to think and pray on that theme as a possible prompt for growth in abiding in our Good God with your life. While doing this, dedicate time to thank Him for the specifics of strengths and weaknesses you might see from this theme as pathways for His work in your life and others.

2. Look up synonyms for "abide" in a book or computer app. Synonyms, or other words with the same/similar meanings, can often bring new connections or ideas to light when you use them in place of a familiar word for something. Say aloud and think on two or three of the synonyms you found for abide that help you better understand the concepts of John chapter 15. Now, write one or more of these synonyms in your calendar for the next two or three weeks as reminders of the need to abide and not hide in your conversations and choices, so as to reflect your growing faith in our Good God at work in your life for His glory and the good of His people.

3. Flashback to elementary or Sunday school projects—if you're able, take a clear glass or plastic cup or container and wash it (if not already clean). Then take a fresh avocado or peach pit and place toothpicks around it to suspend it in fresh water in the cup/container. (Use Google or YouTube for further instructions on this if you haven't seen something like this done before.) Alternatively, take the cup/container with potting soil, moisten the soil, and plant 2-3 bean seeds. Place the cup/container in a

sunny place where you'll see it on a regular basis. As you watch the pit or seeds sprout roots and then a shoot, think about how God is doing a new work for good growth in the soil of your soul. The clear cup/container will also be a reminder of the importance of abiding (and not hiding) and its influence on the health of your relationship with our Good God and His people. A good way to help think on this is to journal your thoughts and pictures of the seeds/pits growing in reflection on the growth occurring in the soil of your soul. Then when the plant is grown, pray about who you can give it to as a reminder to him or her of our Good God's plan and purpose for his or her life to grow and flourish in His love.

"Where are you?" (Genesis 3:9b) questions for this chapter:

1. One of my favorite places in Scripture that refers to home is John 1:14 CEB: *The Word became flesh and made his home among us. We have seen his glory, glory like that of a father's only son, full of grace and truth.* Jesus chose to make His home with us that we might have a forever home with Him (see John 14:3). When was the last time you sat with those verses from John and really looked at your life in light of that truth of home with Christ? What choices did you make today or plans do you have for tomorrow that show the value of abiding and not hiding?

2. Does your calendar or daily planner display Jesus as having made His home here for everyone or just for those in your home or family tree (see John 3:16)? What importance does prayer for your neighbors, community, state, country, and world play in your setting aside time from homework or chores or work or sleep? What importance do those you might never meet in the world have on your budget? Are your choices of purchases for primarily your own home and household, or for theirs to hear and know Jesus' love for them and His making of a forever home for them too?

3. If hiding is your default in having conversations or making community, consider praying for the courage to be brave and abide in our Jesus before the next time you leave the door of your home. Consider putting a sticky note with the word confidence or home on your doorframe to remind you of this truth: God knows all about your fears and already has your day in His plan. This is the time to ask for faith and then to step outside in that faith as your heart abides in the truth that nothing can come between you and our Good God's great love for you (see Romans 8:38-39).

Well Grounded

Reflection prayer:

Dear Father God,

Thank You that You want me to abide in You and with You, wherever You place me in this world. Thank You that You gave Jesus to make His home here for me that I might be able to dwell with You forever. Thank You that You tell me not to be afraid but to be brave and to be like Jesus in the way You made me to be. Please give me the courage to do exactly that today. Please help me to know that You alone are my confidence and my dwelling place for today and the not-yet. Please help me to quiet my heart so that I can hear You tenderly tell me of Your great love for me and for everyone, no matter what any of us have done in days past.

In the strong Name of Jesus,

Amen.

[1]Foster, R.J., 1998. *Streams of Living Water: Celebrating the Great Traditions of Christian Faith,* Harper Collins, San Francisco, CA, p.48.

CULTIVATING
COMMUNITY

*And He said to Adam, "Because you listened to your wife's
voice and ate from the tree about which I commanded you, 'Do
not eat from it': The ground is cursed because of you. You will
eat from it by means of painful labor all the days of your life.
It will produce thorns and thistles for you, and you will eat the
plants of the field. You will eat bread by the sweat of your brow
until you return to the ground, since you were taken from it. For
you are dust, and you will return to dust.*
Genesis 3:17–19 HCSB

In sorrow shalt thou eat.
Genesis 3:17b KJ21

*You will fight for every crumb of food
from the crusty lump of clay I made you from.*
Genesis 3:17b VOICE

Well Grounded

"How we live together may be the greatest sermon we preach"
C. Pohl[1]

The *ground is cursed because of you* – can you imagine how that pronouncement must've felt to Adam? Scripture doesn't tell us his thoughts, but could they have been something like this? To know that he was the source of the curse not only for that which he was tasked to care for and farm, but the very material from which he himself was made. To be the reason that everything he ever walked on, dug up, watered, planted or transplanted in, built on, or washed off was cursed forever. No escape from the outcome of his sin. No release from the implications of one rebellious moment. There was no forgetting that that which used to be under his feet and in his soul was now gone forever.

As a soil scientist and farm girl, Genesis 3:17 is painful deep inside every time I read it. And if I'm reading it aloud, tears can choke me up or escape over the top. That same thick throat happens when I see recent deep gullied-out fields or the eroded soil from them piled up elsewhere. Even if there are signs of the construction or planting to come, the grief and loss of such productivity stabs my heart like seeing a bright student not working at her potential because of poor choices.

And if I react like that, I can't begin to imagine Adam's grief at knowing what he had lost regarding the soil under his feet and in his soul.

Could Adam's tears have put tracks down his face as he watched the cursed ground erode away with waters running in tracks over it instead of into it because it was now hardened? Could his heart have broken even a little more while watching weeds outcompete his crops for precious water, nutrients, and space? Could his soul have been choked even more as he helplessly watched disease and decay overtake roots, shoots, and fruits despite his best attempts with toil, tears, and trembling prayers?

To me, and I think to Adam, soil is far more than what I walk on, dig up, or plant in. Soil is a strong legacy that reaches back to Eden in Genesis and forward to the new earth of Revelation. Soil is a fragile gift handed down in responsibility and rejoicing or in regret from generation to generation. Soil is an expected constant like stars, sky, and seasons, but often overlooked in its innate beauty. Part of the most beautiful and mysterious aspect of soil to me is that just like Adam, I can't make it, but I am inextricably tied to it.

Soil nourishes me, body and soul, in its continual giving and receiving of itself for me. It gives nutrients and water and receives waste. It's a picture of what Jesus does for me every day. He gives the nutrients of love, mercy, grace, hope, joy, strength, and peace to me while receiving the waste of my doubts, fears, anxiety, selfishness, arrogance, distrust, and insecurity. And in His receiving of my waste, He is transforming me into a conduit to bring life to others starving for hope for today and tomorrow (see 2 Corinthians 3:18). All the while, He reminds me of who I truly am and belong to as reflected in Isaiah 64:8 NIV: *Yet You, Lord, are our Father. We are the clay, You are the potter; we are all the work of Your hand.*

As Christians, aren't we to be as soil to others in our lives? To give out the many good gifts we receive from our Good God while being a safe place to receive the unfiltered words or thoughts of those trapped in the waste of sin? To give hope while receiving the harvest of sin in disappointment, hopelessness, discouragement, and despair from others. To receive the waste and to return it as nutrients transformed by trust – both in actions of loving care for them and words of loving truth to them (see 1 John 3:18). We are to give actions in service – seen and unseen. We are to give words of encouragement – in prayer and conversation. (I must remember that listening is a beautiful service of love poured out to and for others.)

Grace is given *to* us for it to be given out *by* us. Grace given in service cultivates community, where community refers to both numbers and maturity of those in the Body of Christ. As Christians, we have been sent into all the world for all time (see Matthew 28:19-20).

God's plan is for everyone to become part of His community of Christ-followers (see 2 Peter 3:9). All of us have been given the gift of Christ. It is our privilege to give of ourselves to others from what He has given for us, that His example might grow out and fill the entire world.

The ones to whom we've been sent to serve are the ones who need us most and need us now. They are the ones who need the grace given and received in what is good and hard, respectively. It's easy to give and receive from those who are grateful, kind, and loving. Such people already have fertile soil in their souls from grace. Yet the ones who aren't easy to love, give, or receive from are the ones whose souls need us to give them what they lack in nutrients of grace, mercy, and love. I think this principle is exemplified in Matthew 25:40 HCSB: *"And the King will answer them, 'I assure you: Whatever you did for one of the least of these brothers of Mine, you did for Me'* and Luke 14:13 CSB: *On the contrary, when you host a banquet, invite those who are poor, maimed, lame, or blind.* Our giving isn't to be reserved to others in the Body of Christ; it's for everyone.

Service done solely for my Savior nourishes the soil of others' souls in the giving and the receiving. Both the giving and the receiving are needed for cultivating community. And both the giving and receiving can be overlooked, unseen, or unknown, like those numerous acts of grace constantly occurring in the soil environment under my feet every day. My acts and words might easily be forgotten or overlooked by all other than the One Who prompted me to do them, as He prepared in advance for me to do (see Ephesians 2:10). Yet those acts and words can prepare the way for greater works which point back to Genesis and forward to Revelation, because they display Jesus as the second Adam (see Romans 5:14 and 1 Corinthians 15:22). My Jesus, the One given to replace sin with righteousness and reunite man with God again (see 1 Corinthians 15:45). For my Jesus is the One Who knows best how and where to cultivate community through gracious service.

The soil environment is a great example of the importance of and need for community. Multiple associations between multiple species of bacteria, fungi, and plants create a place where all can thrive in a soil. Yet if all aren't present, none thrive. Bacteria convert gaseous nitrogen into usable forms and remove waste products. Fungi weave mind-bogglingly large and complex webs between roots and soil particles for nutrient transfer and availability. Plants provide energy sources through root exudates and decay of above-ground materials... each specific to a task, each different in placement and composition, all essential. And if one member of the community struggles, all struggle, because an essential irreplaceable component isn't being provided for another. When relationships like these occur in nature, it's called mutualism – the whole is greater than the sum of the parts.

To take this a bit further, doesn't mutualism sound similar to Paul's description of the early church in 1 Corinthians 12:12-27? All were called. All had different roles, gifts, and positions. All were essential for this community to thrive. And not just to thrive at Corinth, but to overtake the entire world. Not just for those days, but for all days to come, including now. As a member of the Body of Christ and a soil scientist, I long to see thriving communities, both in the soil under my feet and the people in the church. I've been called, equipped, and empowered for service for such communities to flourish in this place at this time (see 1 Corinthians 1:17, Hebrews 4:1, and 1 Peter 2:9). And I think you might realize by now, that you've been called to this too…

Yet all too many times, service in my life looks like Adam's struggle with the soil after Eden. That is, a *fight for every crumb of food from the crusty lump of clay I made you from.* Just like Paul, I war with knowing what I should do and what I'm actually doing (see Galatians 5:17). Or if I am doing what I should, I still battle with having a right attitude in the doing. Geeky me compares this idea to that of the soil texture of a loam. The perceived ideal soil texture of a true loam only exists if made in a laboratory. Loams are looked for in nature but rarely found. Similarly, my ideal acts of service that I've made in the laboratory of my mind are for me, not for my Jesus. Such acts are meant for others to see me, not for them to find Jesus. Thus, the ongoing battle between what I'm doing versus what He wants me to do. And all of this is because the soil of my soul needs to be rebuilt into the Image of my Jesus. Because if not, it will just keep producing *thorns and thistles.* The cursed ground of the soil of my soul has the natural tendency to sin, despite my best efforts otherwise. But there is hope as seen in 1 Corinthians 15:49 EHV: *And just as we have borne the image of the man made of dust, we will also bear the image of the heavenly man.* Jesus can and will do the very good work of transforming me from the cursed ground up and out.

He alone can do a full-blown metamorphosis of the soil of my soul. Not just in words on a page, but in focus, thought patterns, responses, choices, and identity as humble obedience. And for this soil scientist, humble obedience is easily not my first, second, third, or any choice. Yet I know it is essential if I want my default to be something other than Isaiah 29:16 CSB: *You have turned things around, as if the potter were the same as the clay. How can what is made say about its maker, "He didn't make me?" How can what is formed say about the one who formed it, "He doesn't understand what he's doing?"* I may not say those questions aloud, but my choices proclaim them, independent of circumstances in my life. Circumstances shouldn't control my choices. Right choices remain right, even when circumstances change. Even the best circumstances cannot produce best choices if the soil of my soul isn't being transformed to be like my Christ.

I see this principle displayed in that even with ideal soil, weather, seeds, fertilizer, labor, and timing, successful harvests require pain, struggle, sorrow, prayer, and toil. Similarly, even with those acts of service that cause my soul to soar, I must pay the costs of time, energy, saying no to other opportunities, and trusting obedience. And these costs, especially in the choosing of trusting obedience, can require suffering in the waiting, longing, and wondering. Suffering is definitely not a first choice for this soil scientist. Yet Scripture tells me Jesus had to learn trusting obedience through suffering (see Hebrews 5:8 in the Message version). So, why am I repeatedly surprised that I must also learn trusting obedience? This principle is even more foundationally true when I'm not seeing the people I'm called to serve through the lens of love. If I'm picking and choosing the people, acts, or circumstances of service that seem easy, fulfilling, quick, or inexpensive, then I'm thinking and showing that my way is better than my Good God's choice for community. Those harder-to-love people or harder-to-do acts are often the ones God has called me to choose. His way is counter-cultural; His way is eternal. He wants community, while I want completion of this task and to move on to something more appealing. (Classic example: I think Jesus would've volunteered for nursery duty every Sunday at my church. He'd change those diapers with a smile and a song, instead of watching the clock and hoping for an early dismissal.) Every time I choose to see me instead of Jesus, I'm ignoring or rejecting that He's made me to be a vital part of community *how* I am, *where and when* I am, and *with* those around me. Or in soil science speak, I'm trying to be a plant, bacteria, or soil particle when He's made me to be a fungus.

Growing up reading missionary biographies reinforced the idea I learned in gardening: much planting, cultivating, watering, fertilizing, and watching is required for fruit production. Years, decades, and generations can pass without much or even any visible fruit. Yet God knows, tends, and nurtures both the seeds and their planters in the silent times. And when God deems it to be springtime, a solid, stable, and substantial joy will bloom in lives forever changed by the Gospel, having been watered by tears of loss, sacrifice, prayers, and waiting. Such stories mirror those found in Scripture, growing faith in the soil of souls like mine. I'm not one who naturally waits patiently for fruit like the farmer in James 5:7. Yet I'm (slowly) learning that the work of waiting (intercession, meditation, attending) produces fruit in my life and others, even if I may not see it. A legacy of faith-seeds for the next generation is priceless, especially as our world grows darker and our time shorter. For when faith-seeds like these are planted and given the time to grow deep roots and strong shoots, they will produce abundant and sweet fruit like no other. Fruit that in turn will produce many strong and vibrant faith-seeds for generations to come, in these fields and others not yet even dreamed of or imagined (see Ephesians 3:20-21).

Some are called to plant or water, others to weed or fertilize, and still others to harvest (see John 4:34-38). Some tasks are recognized, while many are not. Yet all people and all tasks are important, essential, and seen by our Good God. All are necessary for a harvest of souls living in the now and not-yet on this cursed ground under our feet. All are necessary for a harvest of souls living without hope in the *dust* of their souls which bear only *thorns and thistles* because they don't know or trust our Good God. Now is our time for trusting obedience and active service to cultivate the community described in Revelation 7:9-10 ESV: *After this I looked, and behold, a great multitude that no one could number, from every nation, from all tribes and peoples and languages, standing before the throne and before the Lamb, clothed in white robes, with palm branches in their hands and crying out with a loud voice, "Salvation belongs to our God who sits on the throne, and to the Lamb!".*

Cultivating Community

Cultivating community requires far more of me than I'm naturally inclined to give. It requires my Jesus actively working in and through me to transform every particle of me into desiring what He has planned for me with others. To love them as He does and to extend that same grace and mercy given to me requires His supernatural strength and power alive in me. Thanks be to God, He can and will do this in ways far better and more than I could hope for.

Take some time to look up, write out, and meditate on each of the Scriptures in this chapter, presented in order of appearance.

1. Genesis 3:17-19
2. 2 Corinthians 3:18

3. Isaiah 64:8
4. 1 John 3:18
5. Matthew 28:19-20
6. 2 Peter 3:9
7. Matthew 25:40
8. Luke 14:13
9. Ephesians 2:10
10. Romans 5:14
11. 1 Corinthians 15:22 and 15:45
12. 1 Corinthians 12:12-27
13. 1 Corinthians 1:17
14. Hebrews 4:1
15. 1 Peter 2:9
16. Galatians 5:17
17. 1 Corinthians 15:49
18. Isaiah 29:16
19. Hebrews 5:8 (preferably in the Message version)
20. James 5:7
21. Ephesians 3:20-21
22. John 4:34-38
23. Revelation 7:9-10 (best if read aloud and more than once)

Questions to consider:

Which of these verses nourished the soil of your soul today
with hope, joy, courage, or faith?

Did any of these verses remind you of other Scripture passages or stories which made you stop and think about the status of the soil of your soul? If so, then list the other passages or stories and their importance to your life today.

Which of these verses (the ones in this chapter or ones you were reminded of) could be helpful to someone else in your life today? Take some time to send a verse or two to a friend in a text, email, note, or card. Not only will the other person be helped by this act, so will you as the writing of the verse(s) will again reinforce truth and right thinking in your mind and the soil of your soul.

Which of these verses do you need to write on a card or to-do list to come back to again tomorrow (and days again afterwards) for more reflection, prayer, and reframing of your perspective as to align your heart with His?

Exercises to do:

1. Purchase or obtain a tree seedling or a perennial plant. If you are able, plant it somewhere you can see it regularly, but not in your own yard or garden. If it's in a pot, plan on transplanting it outside at the appropriate time where it can keep growing when it gets too big for the pot. Check Google

for the appropriate planting time for your region and climate. Calendar this time (day or week) on your phone or planner so you won't forget to put your plant or seedling into the ground. Also, google best practices for planting your seedling or plant – including such things as if you need to add fertilizer into the hole before the plant, cutting holes in the burlap around the root ball, watering schedule after planting, and such. And even better, refer to exercise 3 to do this with and for friends – talk about a great way to invite others to join you in community, both inside and outside the Body of Christ!

2. Maybe your neighbor would enjoy a similar seedling or plant in his or her yard, flower bed, or apartment balcony or garden area? What about someone who is homebound, disabled, or elderly and might feel overlooked by the community? A plant or seedling could serve as a visible reminder that they are loved or known. Calendar future visits with them for transplanting the seedling or plant with the directions you've googled above for your own plant. And when you go to work, make sure and allow time for conversation (especially the part of listening on your end).

3. Consider doing this exercise on a bigger scale for some place in your community – school, church, park, or recreation area – so that others can benefit from seeing beauty in the trees or perennial plants. Activities like these are best done with others and can be great ways to build friendships, both in the work together and in seeing the lasting results in days to come. Regular scheduling of weeding, fertilizing, and mulching is a great way to involve people who couldn't come to the initial planting, as well as a great way to make this a regular discipline more than a one-time event. Plus, these less glamorous, less immediately fulfilling, or often-overlooked tasks are no less important than the work of planting. They can serve as a step in your learning to choose such kinds of tasks for your community and for your family, too. Repeated care like this also shows the commitment to community and the value of investment over time as looking towards eternity. My church has done similar things for a couple of local schools, with great results of families hearing about Christ and His love for them who might never have heard otherwise.

"Where are you?" (Genesis 3:9b) questions for this chapter:

1. List the ways you're serving others – be it in your family, neighborhood, workplace, church, or community. Mark the ways you delight in with a star. Mark the ways where you see God at work with a cross. Mark the ways in which your life is being changed through service with a heart. Now take some time to thank God for all of these ways you love Him by serving others. Pray for each of the activities you marked with a star, then those with a cross, then those with a heart, and finally, those you didn't mark at all. Pray especially for those that aren't marked and for the people involved in them with you. Ask God to open your eyes to see beneath the surface into what He's doing in all of these places, especially those which aren't marked.

2. If you're not actively involved in service right now, take some time to pray and seek our Good God for His direction as to where He has for you to love Him through loving people in service. He has a purpose, plan, and place to each and every one of us. Now is a great time to find that place and worship Him there!

3. Consider making these reflections a regular part of your calendar year (starting now and looking

forward, not waiting until January 1ˢᵗ). Consider repeating them every three or four months to watch how God is working in and through you, for others and with Him, in His great love for them and you.

Reflection prayer:

Dear Father,

Thank You that You have a plan for grace and for community for my life with others. Thank You that You put opportunities in my day to cultivate my relationship with You as I cultivate my time and tasks with and for others. Please help me to stop, see, and listen to You and to Your people, all of them, especially those who might be in the background. Please help me to love others as You love them and me.

In the strong Name of Jesus,

Amen.

[1]Pohl, Christian as quoted in J.W. Earley. 2019. "The Common Rule: Habits of Purpose for an Age of Distraction", InterVarsity Press, Downers Grove, IL. p. 58.

Well Grounded

CULTIVATING
CONTENTMENT

*God, you are my God. I want to follow you. My whole being
thirsts for you, like a man in a dry, empty land where there is no
water. I have seen you in the Temple. I have seen your strength
and glory. Your love is better than life. I will praise you. I will
praise you as long as I live. I will lift up my hands in prayer to
your name. I will be content as if I had eaten the best foods. My
lips will sing. My mouth will praise you.*
Psalm 63:1–5 ICB

*Then the LORD God took the man and put him in the Garden
of Eden to cultivate it and tend it.*
Genesis 2:15 NASB

*"Acts of gratitude make one grateful because,
step by step, they reveal that all is grace."*
H. Nouwen[1]

"Give thanks"[2]

Give thanks with a grateful heart
Give thanks to the Holy One
Give thanks because He's given
Jesus Christ, His Son

And now let the weak say, "I am strong"
Let the poor say, "I am rich"
Because of what the Lord has done for us

Give thanks
We give thanks (give thanks)
We give thanks

Every time I thought or prayed about how to write this chapter, that song came to mind. And many of those times, I found myself singing it aloud in expression of how much I do long for a *grateful heart*. God tells us in Psalm 100:1 that He welcomes those out-of-key, missing a word or three, joyful noises offered in worship like I bring to Him. For me, joy is usually in its own key not found in a music book or choir special. The lyrics of "Give Thanks" are not directly from Scripture, but the essence of them encapsulates Psalm 63:1-5. Psalm 42:1-2 AMP also captures this idea with: *As the deer pants [longingly] for the water brooks, So my soul pants [longingly] for You, O God. My soul (my life, my inner self) thirsts for God, for the living God. When will I come and see the face of God?*

For the truth is that only when I see His face am I whole and thus, truly contented.

I long for Him to cultivate gratitude deep in the soil of my soul. There, it softens and strengthens my choices for contentment, along with changing me more into the Image of my Jesus. I long for Him to plant and nurture a deep hunger for nothing other than obedience to God and His presence in my days, in both familiar and remarkable ways. In other words, I long to recognize, revel, and revere Him in that work done in, for, and through my life for His glory and the good of His people in His time and way(s). I long for Him to grow that unmistakable, irreplaceable longing satisfied only with His good love all through the morning, noon, and nights of the days set for me (see Psalm 90:14 and Job 14:5).

Cultivation isn't an immediate, simple, or easy process; it's a necessary one.

With that in mind, could the process of cultivating contentment in my life be similar to the events in Genesis 2:15? God planted Eden. God brought Adam to Eden. God assigned Eden to Adam. God appointed Adam as caretaker of Eden. Eden had it all, and in spades, if you will. Therefore, Adam had access to it all, except one tree (see Genesis 2:16-17). But Scripture also tells us that the rest of Eden wasn't enough for Adam; he had to have that one forbidden tree (see Genesis 3:6). Adam wasn't content with his portion in Eden; he had to have it all.

In assigning Adam as caretaker of Eden, could God have also been assigning him to be a caretaker of contentment in his own life? To choose to be content, fully satisfied with the abundance assigned to him, like David was in Psalm 16:6 NIV: *The boundary lines have fallen for me in pleasant places; surely I have a delightful inheritance?* Similarly, has God appointed me to be a caretaker of the gratitude God has planted in the soil of my soul? God prepared Eden for Adam and Adam for Eden. Then God put Adam in Eden with the task of caring for it. More specifically, Adam's task was to tend, watch over, and guard Eden as if he were performing religious duties in worship of God, like the Levite priests did with the tabernacle. The verbs "cultivate" and "tend" in the Hebrew in Genesis 2:15 are the same words used with the Levites' tabernacle and temple duties later in the Old Testament.[3] (Stop and hold that thought close and cherish it for a minute or two. We'll return to this idea soon.)

God provided everything needed for the Levites to do their task – the design, details, and directions of and for the tabernacle and then, the temple (see Exodus chapters 25-31 and 1 Kings 5-6). Nothing was overlooked. It was all there, be it materials, artisans, or the desire of the people to participate in His plan. God wasn't just involved in the building of the tabernacle and the temple, but in the keeping of them. He appointed the Levites, a people set aside by God for care of the tabernacle and later, the temple. Just like He did with Eden and Adam years before.

Everything was there for Adam's assignment as husbandman of the pre-heaven of Eden and his own heart. And God has done the same for me today. He's provided everything for me, here and now, to be a husbandman of contentment in my life.

Husbandman isn't a commonly used term, even in the King James Version of Scripture. It's only referenced seven times; none of which refer to Adam.[4] Yet the essence of a husbandman is seen in Genesis 2:15 in Adam's cultivating and tending of Eden as if performing religious duties to God in worship. For as a husband is to tenderly love, care for, and protect his wife in Ephesians 5:25, so a husbandman does with those under his care, be they plant, animal, water, air, or soil. A husbandman obedient to his God is distinctive in his approach as a faithful, careful, and patient steward of resources for current and future needs. He is humble, watchful, and diligent. He tends for all and for each under his care, like with the shepherd who left the 99 to go after the one (see Luke 15:4).

A husbandman's role sounds like what I'm commanded to do about contentment in such verses as Proverbs 4:23 GW: *Guard your heart more than anything else, because the source of your life flows from it*; 2 Corinthians 12:10 ESV: *For the sake of Christ, then, I am content with weaknesses, insults, hardships, persecutions, and calamities. For when I am weak, then*

I am strong; and Hebrews 13:5 EHV: *Keep your life free from the love of money, and be content with what you have. For God has said: I will never leave you, and I will never forsake you.* I am tasked to watch, keep, trust, and stay here in what God has given for this time and place in His plan for me (see Proverbs 3:5-6). He has given me the duty of cultivating the soil of my soul for a good harvest of gratitude in all circumstances, at all times (see 1 Thessalonians 5:18 and Acts 24:3). He has promised to work everything out for good (see Romans 8:28). So, if everything is prepared and provided for me as seen in Matthew 6:33, this job should be simple and easy, right? Yet, for me (and possibly for Adam), it is (was) a constant struggle against self.

This duty is hard because a husbandman of contentment recognizes that discontent is disguised pride. And disguised pride feeds the lie that what I think I should have in my life is better than what God has provided. Bottom line: if Eden wasn't enough for Eve or Adam, nothing will ever be enough for discontented me. "Just one more" always demands far more than I have to give. Yearning for that accolade or accomplishment, outfit or opportunity, habit or house is another bite of the apple that has already separated me from the everyday Eden God has planted for and placed me in, here and now.

The garden of gratitude He has planted in the soil of my soul withers with every moment I encourage envy instead of cultivating contentment. For example, even now, discontent has me by the throat in demanding that I email a publisher to see his decision on a book; check the statistics on my blog to see if someone else has signed up to follow it; or leave here and go to the store (or online) to shop for yet another cute little thing. None of these actions bring rest for my soul; all drain away peace like a sieve.

In contrast, when I cultivate contentment, I harvest grace. For gratitude gives me the right lens to see the fruit of Spirit-led sanctification flourishing in my life – the *love, joy, peace, patience, kindness, goodness, faithfulness, gentleness,* [and] *self-control* of Galatians 5:22-23 ESV. All of this is grace! The opposite of the death I deserve for what I've done – a very good grace for this moment of growing here in the Eden of the everyday with Jesus. The everyday that started at salvation and extends into eternity – such grace!

And this grace is real, lasting, and strong. Strong enough to teach and then remind me that cultivating contentment is worth every battle waged against self. For grace is my most effective tool to weed out discontent, replant gratitude, and build garden walls to keep out arrogance.

Garden walls are vital for my role as a husbandman of contentment so I can stand on them and see far off what's coming to prepare for it (see Ezekiel 3:17). Choices such as irrigating humility in preparation for that accolade or accomplishment so that God receives the credit, not me; fertilizing love in preparation for giving the money instead of buying the outfit or opportunity; and disking in diligence in preparation to faithfully work on that habit or house to make it a blessing for others. I must be that watchman on the wall so this grace will thrive. For only God's grace can convert discontent's fodder into a harvest of grace in my life for His glory and the good of His people.

Talking about cultivating contentment and actively doing it are not the same. I can write all day about how wonderful grace is, but we all know talk is cheap. 2 Corinthians 10:5 GNT: *we pull down every proud obstacle that is raised against the knowledge of God; we take every thought captive and make it obey Christ* -- this is where I must dwell. I must choose to abide in the truth that what God has here for me will always be enough. The grace of this moment will ever be enough, especially when self is standing up and shaking her fist at unanswered questions, prayers, or dreams. But hallelujah! When God is here in the grace of this moment, He alone is enough to speak a quiet peace louder than the screams of the lie that I am not enough.

Just like how Adam and Eve believed that lie of not enough, I do too. For contentment to truly be cultivated and cherished in this moment of grace, that lie has to be dug out of the bedrock of the soil of my soul. I must choose truth in all ways, including and especially through deciding beforehand not to dig in the quicksand of media, social and otherwise. Media wants me to believe that contentment isn't attainable, except through getting just one more thing and then I'll be "enough." Cultivating contentment demands that I find my worth and satisfaction in God alone. I'll never be enough or have enough outside of my Good God. And from this soil scientist who's tried a whole bunch of stuff other than Scripture to find contentment (and failed), that's the truth!

Truth and lies cannot coexist. And this is truth - only my God is the true Rock that is higher than I (see Psalm 62:1). For *there is no rock like our God* (1 Samuel 2:2b ESV).

This God is the One Who calls me to cultivate contentment in the soil of my soul, like He did Adam with Eden. He has graciously prepared, provided, planted, and placed me in the garden of today. He has called me like the Levites to worship Him in the duties of watching, working, and waiting for His leading, in the enough of His plan for me for here today. This is my proper response – "A quiet heart is content with what God gives. It is enough. All is Grace."[5]

Cultivating Contentment

Cultivating contentment goes against my natural inclinations for me. Whether or not all in life is as I'd hoped, deep down the lie that I'm not enough demands more and more to try and quiet it. Yet my Good Gardener God doesn't let me struggle on my own. The Holy Spirit is within me, and Jesus prays for me with a power and strength far greater than any lie or temptation. Contentment isn't reserved for someone else; Jesus can make it a reality for me in the grace of today.

Take some time to look up, write out, and meditate on each of the Scriptures in this chapter, presented in order of appearance.

1. Psalm 63:1-5
2. Genesis 2:15-17
3. Psalm 100:1
4. Psalm 42:1-2
5. Psalm 90:14
6. Job 14:5
7. Genesis 3:6
8. Psalm 16:6
9. Exodus 25-31
10. 1 Kings 5-6
11. Ephesians 5:25
12. Luke 15:4
13. Proverbs 4:23
14. 2 Corinthians 12:10
15. Hebrews 13:5
16. Proverbs 3:5-6
17. 1 Thessalonians 5:18
18. Acts 24:3
19. Romans 8:28
20. Matthew 6:33
21. Galatians 5:22-23

22. Ezekiel 3:17
23. 2 Corinthians 10:5
24. Psalm 62:1
25. 1 Samuel 2:2

Questions to consider:

Which of these verses nourished the soil of your soul today with hope, joy, courage, or faith?

Did any of these verses remind you of other Scripture passages or stories which made you stop and think about the status of the soil of your soul? If so, then list the other passages or stories and their importance to your life today.

Which of these verses (the ones in this chapter or ones you were reminded of) could be helpful to someone else in your life today? Take some time to send a verse or two to a friend in a text, email, note, or card. Not only will the other person be helped by this act, so will you as the writing of the verse(s) will again reinforce truth and right thinking in your mind and the soil of your soul.

Which of these verses do you need to write on a card or to-do list to come back to again tomorrow (and days again afterwards) for more reflection, prayer, and reframing of your perspective as to align your heart with His?

Exercises to do:

1. If possible, go for a walk outside. Take two bags with you – one for trash and one for treasures. As you walk, pick up any trash you see and put it in the trash bag. Do the same with any treasures you see (pretty leaves, rocks, branches, feathers, etc. or something that was discarded as trash but that you can use in your home – a good box or container, etc.). While you are walking and looking, express gratitude to God for the ability to walk, the place to walk, the bounty you find, and the people who have put out what they considered trash. Pray that God would help you and them to replace the lie deep inside that you are trash with the truth that we are all treasures in the sight of God. Thank God that He sees you and everyone as precious and loved in being blessed with much grace.

2. If you are in the process of (or thinking about doing) a clean-out and reorganization of your home, thank God for the bounty He has given in full closets, drawers, and rooms. Gratitude can turn a daunting or distasteful task into praise. Praise Him one drawer or closet at a time (all of it doesn't have to be done today!). Ask Him to use this bounty to bless others as you are packing it up to get rid of it. Ask Him to

replace the lie of "more" with the truth that all is grace while you are loading it in your vehicle(s) to donate. Pray to find the specific places where this bounty can be used for God's glory and the good of His people. Have you thought about donating luggage, toys, baby stuff, or kids' clothes to foster care? Have you considered asking your church about a clothes closet or free garage "sale" for neighbors in need? Have you considered using extra foodstuffs for homeless shelters? There are so many possibilities with ideas from prayer! And the joy from praise gives fresh strength to open the next door and tackle the next pile.

3. Whenever you will be receiving or requesting items, new or used (such as the holidays, inheriting a parent's or grandparent's home and its contents, or setting up a registry for a wedding, new home, or baby, for instance) consider stepping back and seeing these items in a new way. Instead of seeing what needs to be gotten rid of, or bought, or replaced with something better, thank God for what is in front of you. And then pray for creativity to better use what God has already given. Do you see these items as part of the *pleasant places* our Good God has drawn out for you (Psalm 16:6 NIV)? Or do you see them as a burden (inheritance of excess) or as deserved (nice wedding gifts)? Could they be given

away or sold to help someone else? The term "living life with open hands" can be especially applicable here. Full hearts are not from full closets or homes; full hearts overflow from grace. The grace of this moment here in the Presence of God.

"Where are you?" (Genesis 3:19) questions for this chapter:

1. How would you rate the contentment level in your life today? 1 being "utterly discontent with everything and everyone in your life" and 10 being "overwhelmed with the goodness of God in the abundance of all of your life". Write your answer and today's date here: _____

2. List 2-3 adjectives to describe your thoughts about David's description of his life in Psalm 16:6. Do you wish you could use his words to describe your life today? Why or why not?

3. Google the lyrics to Rich Mullins' song called "My One Thing". Now listen to this song on YouTube, Spotify, or elsewhere while reading the lyrics to it. Afterwards, take a minute or two to write down your gut response to this song. What does your life look like in comparison to the thoughts contained in this song?

If you're anything like me, this chapter needs another read-through with prayer. Cultivating contentment is a very good work that must be done carefully and consistently. Just like cleaning or cleaning out isn't a one-shot deal, contentment requires constant care and commitment. One small step towards Jesus in contentment can harvest much grace for today, and again tomorrow.

Reflection prayer:

Dear Father God,

Thank You for putting me here in this Eden of the everyday. Thank You for how You've crafted it for me and me for it, with purpose and a plan for good. Thank You that You're preparing a far better garden for all of us for eternity with You in heaven one day. Please help me to find my delight and rest in You alone, for that is true contentment. Please help me to desire only what You have deemed best for me and to trust You fully in that choice.

In the strong Name of Jesus,

Amen.

[1]Nouwen, Henri. 1992. "The Return of the Prodigal Son", Doubleday, Image Books, New York, NY. p. 85.

[2]"Give Thanks" written by Henry Smith, sung by Don Moen, released 1990.

[3]Wenham, Gordon J. 1987. Word Biblical Commentary: Genesis 1-15. D.A. Hubbard and G.W. Barker, General Editors. Zondervan, Grand Rapids, MI. p. 67.

[4]https://www.biblegateway.com as referenced on 1/20/22 for word search on husbandman in KJV.

[5]Elliot, Elisabeth. 1995. "Keep a Quiet Heart", Vine Books, Servant Publishing, Ann Arbor, MI.

CULTIVATING
CRYING OUT

*Yet day by day the Lord also pours out his steadfast love
upon me, and through the night I sing his songs and pray
to God who gives me life.*
Psalm 42:8 TLB

*"To pray is to change...the closer we come to the heartbeat
of God, the more we see our need and the more we desire
to be conformed to Christ."*
R.J. Foster[1]

One of the best principles I learned from my parents
and grandparents was that prayer is essential to life:
for farming, friendships, family, teaching, trials, tempta-

tions, and everything in between. I have many memories of my parents and grandparents praying. They prayed for family, friends, finances, freedom, and the farm, just to name a few. They asked with bold expectation; they thanked with grateful hearts. But always, they prayed with humility, tied to their Savior in their hearts and the soil under their feet.

A common request I remember them praying for was rain, specifically a good "farmer's rain." A long, steady, slow shower that drenches soil and soul in its gift of life-giving water and nutrients.

This farmer's daughter knows full well, like Elijah did in 1 Kings 18:44, the gift of a good rain. Not even the best irrigation systems can replace a good rain. For the gift of one is far bigger than the volume of the water itself. Rain freshens with nutrients returned from air to ground and awakens sleeping roots, bacteria, fungi, and other vital soil residents. Rain cleans atmospheres above and below the soil surface while restoring pathways for nutrient transformation and transport. A good rain is a good gift from our Good God.

The benefits of a good rain can't be duplicated by irrigation or any type of management choice. A good rain can only be prayed and hoped for as a good gift from our Good God. Thus, the appropriate position for a farmer to receive the gift of a good rain is on her knees. Likewise, the appropriate position for a farmer's daughter to receive an answered prayer is on her knees. Neither a good rain nor a prayer's answer can be replicated; it can only be received. And it can only be received with open hands, hearts, minds, and eyes watching the heavens in expectation of more rain and more answered prayers to come at the right time (see James 5:7).

I wonder if Adam thought like this about prayer? Scripture doesn't tell us that he knew the gift of a good rain, since the first rain isn't mentioned until Genesis 7:4 (see also Genesis 2:5). Yet as the world's first farmer, he must have known about the essential nature of water for people, plants, and animals. Did he know long days when all was dry and hard? Were there days he cried out for water to bring life to the dust under his feet and in his soul? Did these prayers come one after another like the breath in and out from his lungs? Could he have prayed something like this? "Please God, I need water for the crops to feed my family. I need the refreshing that I used to know in my times with You in Eden. I have been working hard on this cursed ground; I am so thirsty and out of breath."

With those thoughts in mind, could Adam himself be a picture for us of a life of prayer? For Adam was a man of dust with the breath of God put in him, working cursed ground in the hope of feeding his family. He had to have known he was dependent on God's provision, breath and water included. And that's what I am too – a [wo]man of dust walking on cursed ground, trying to breathe in and out prayers to my Jesus, the hope of glory, Who remembers that I am but dust and gives rain in due time (see Colossians 1:27, Psalm 103:14, and Hebrews 6:7). And I don't think I'm alone in this awareness of dust, breath, rain, and long days full of hard work on cursed ground.

As one who's lived in and through many dry, dusty days without rain or relief, where prayers were as numerous as breath, I think that Adam might have known and embraced the power of prayer after Eden. Could prayers have been as breath for him too? Could the people of Israel in the drought of 1 Kings 8 have tasted this kind of life in a deep thirst – both in their hearts from sin and their mouths from no rain for drinking water? (Please stop and take a minute or two to read the story of Elijah and a long-awaited rain in 1 Kings chapters 17 and 18. And while you're reading, be sure and savor a good glass of clean, cold water.)

Now that you're refreshed, body and soul, from drinking deep from Scripture and your glass, let's savor another idea on breath and life and our Good God. Our Good God is the only One Who can provide all we yearn for or need at any moment, be it water, life, or breath. Let's stop here for a breath or two and ponder this:

This breath in can be a prayer.
That breath out, yet another prayer.

Oswald Chambers captures this idea with "If we think of prayer as the breath in our lungs…we think rightly."[2]

Those afflicted with lung conditions often use moisture in the form of steam and drinking lots of water to help loosen dry tissues for deeper breathing. I think the same idea of needing water can apply here about prayer: water for my dry heart in a drought of self-imposed separation from my Good God. The good gift of a good rain of restoration can only come from my Good God when I choose confession and repentance in prayer. And many times, those kind of prayers are ones I can only breathe in and out through a rain of tears down my face.

Each breath can be a prayer to our Good God, Who breathed life into Adam and does the same for me, even now (see Psalm 150:6). This thought makes the *pray without ceasing* of 1 Thessalonians 5:17 ESV become alive and real to me in this moment, in this breath. Every breath can be an acknowledgement that I cannot, but God can and will. Each breath can be an autonomic realignment of my life by the prayer from my lungs out to my God. The next breath is then a natural response to my Creator God of prayer via a fundamental innate and inherent mechanism of anatomy and physiology. One breath can be a literal return of prayer and praise to my God.

What is needed for life for me in breath can bring life to me in prayer.

Psalm 8:2 CEV expands on this idea: *With praises from children and from tiny infants, you have built a fortress. It makes your enemies silent, and all who turn against you are left speechless.* This breath, this praise, this prayer can be a piece of the fortress God has built and holds against whatever enemy is trying to flood my life with temptation, even now. My Sovereign God stands firm, holds fast, and gives life, breath, joy, faith, hope, and strength (see Colossians 1:11). He is the strong tower I can run to and be saved (see Proverbs 18:10). Nothing can stand against God, even that next step or breath which seems insurmountable in days full of dust without rain (see Luke 1:37).

On that note, could Adam's heart and mind have been full of cloudy memories of the once-was Eden mixed with the rainy tears of the now-cursed ground of regret and remorse? Could these memories have been reinforced with every washing of his body or of the now-dead animal skins he wore to cover his shame? For not even water in abundance or the deepest of breaths could wash or blow away what he'd done and its effect on his children, grandchildren, and onwards to us here in the dust of today (see Exodus 20:5).

Yet, today and every day, I am given opportunity for confession, repentance, and receiving forgiveness that washes away all sin (see 1 John 1:9). No sin is exempt from the gift of Calvary; no one is beyond the grace of the Cross. When I came for salvation nearly 50 years ago, I was washed clean. When I come today for repentance, I receive new waters of grace that restore, renew, and welcome me to walk again with my God until my return to dust, His appearing, or until I am simply no longer here, like Enoch (see Genesis 5:24). (Oh Jesus, please help me to have such a close walk with and constant prayer to You that my life would remind others of the closeness Enoch shared with You.)

Like rain, prayer is a process pointing to and leading towards God. Like rain, prayer is from God. The Holy Spirit prompts the prayer. Jesus prepares the way for the prayer and pray-er. God provides an answer to the prayer of the pray-er. For example, have you ever had someone keep coming to mind with a certain need that you had never thought of before for them? And when you cry out for this need for this person, the hair on your arms or neck stands up, and you know deep inside that this was what you were supposed to pray for them at this time and in this way? Then later, you find out your prayer was spot-on in request and timing, even if it may have seemed outlandish or far-fetched when you prayed it. If so, then you have experienced the process of prayer made manifest by our Good God's power.

Effective praying is not just scattering fairy dust across my life or another's. It is words, love, time, effort, faith, focus, and trust given in a rain of hope. Prayer is a dedicated gift of breath and life to the God Who already knows the situation and will exert His power for what is best to happen. Effective pray-ers do make things happen, according to James 5:16b HCSB, which says, *the urgent request of a righteous person is very powerful in its effect.* Effective prayers and pray-ers are persistent, passionate, and powerful pursuits and pursuers of God's glory, His righteousness, and His kingdom (see Matthew 6:33).

The process of effective praying not only waters the dust of another's soul and life; it does the same for me. Sometimes, I don't realize just how dusty my own life is until I jump into the waters of prayer for a family member, friend, colleague, or someone I don't know living across the world from me. Prayer reminds me that I'm Adam's child. Yet, prayer also reminds me that I am a daughter of the King, called, equipped, and sent to proclaim hope to the dead men walking around me (see Galatians 4:7, Ephesians 2:10, and Matthew 28:18-20).

Effective prayers and pray-ers are not one-time flood events. They can continue for years, seemingly without much to show for them or their lives. Yet, at the right time, God will make things happen (and quickly), according to Isaiah 60:22b CEV which says, *I am the LORD, and when the time comes, I will quickly do all this.* A great example of this was Elijah, who prayed for three years for no rain. Therefore, there wasn't just dust, but drought throughout the land, lives, and hearts of those living there. Likewise, when it was time, God told Elijah to pray for rain, and voilà: a torrent of rain starting from *a cloud as small as a man's hand* (1 Kings 18:44 HCSB and see James 5:17-18).

Just as that next breath may be a fight for one with lung disease, so might be that next prayer offered by that pray-er fighting doubt, fear, or pride. Or that pray-er trying to pause amidst a full calendar, list, home, or office. Or that pray-er rejecting the crushing inadequacy of past mistakes or present expectations. As one who's been beaten and left face-down by all those challenges, I can say with confidence that God knows, God hears, and God answers as only God can. My job is to listen.

God gives the listening pray-er the breath and the prayer. And He gives the listening pray-er the strength to breathe the prayer with full expectation of Him opening the floodgates of powerful answering. Whether the powerful answering is a challenge conquered or a peace in that furnace or lions' den, God gives Himself to the pray-er in ways beyond understanding or imagination of the prayer given (see Ephesians 3:20-21 and Isaiah 55:8-9). God calls all of us to prayer as pray-ers who love Him and thus, love others in prayer. And here in the dust of today, God can and will bring us showers of hope for now and for eternity as described in Psalm 113:4-9 MSG:

> GOD *is higher than anything and anyone, outshining everything you can see in the skies. Who can compare with* GOD, *our God, so majestically enthroned, Surveying his magnificent heavens and earth? He picks up the poor from out of the [dust], rescues the forgotten who've been thrown out with the trash, Seats them among the honored guests, a place of honor among the brightest and best. He gives childless couples a family, gives them joy as the parents of children. Hallelujah!*

Cultivating Crying Out

Cultivating crying out to my Good God should be easier than I make it out to be. Breathing is (normally) something I don't have to think about; crying out should be like that in every situation. This breath offered to God in praise for this goodness in front of me. The next breath given to God in supplication for this person or this particular situation in front of me. Those words, those thoughts sent in straight lines to my Good God, almost like the waterfall of raindrops running down my office windowpane right now. Anything can serve as a prompt to prayer; everything can be a reminder of the need for prayer. Only our Good God has the power and authority to radically change our world one moment or one person at a time. And that person can be us! Our Good God has given us the continual opportunity to cry out to Him for this moment and this person at any time and in any place. He's always listening to us; let's be always crying out to Him.

Take some time to look up, write out, and meditate on each of the Scriptures in this chapter, presented in order of appearance.

1. Psalm 4:28
2. 1 Kings 18:44
3. James 5:7
4. Genesis 7:4
5. Genesis 2:5

6. Colossians 1:27
7. Psalm 103:14 and 150:6
8. Hebrews 6:7
9. 1 Kings 8
10. 1 Kings 17–18
11. Leviticus 26:4
12. 1 Thessalonians 5:17
13. Psalm 8:2
14. Colossians 1:11
15. Proverbs 18:10
16. Luke 1:37
17. Exodus 20:5
18. 1 John 1:9
19. Genesis 5:24
20. James 5:16–18
21. Matthew 6:33
22. Galatians 4:7
23. Ephesians 2:10
24. Matthew 28:18–20
25. Isaiah 60:22
26. James 5:17–18
27. Ephesians 3:20–21
28. Isaiah 55:8–9
29. Psalm 113:4–9

Questions to consider:

Which of these verses nourished the soil of your soul today with hope, joy, courage, or faith?

Did any of these verses remind you of other Scripture passages or stories which made you stop and think about the status of the soil of your soul? If so, then list the other passages or stories and their importance to your life today.

Which of these verses (the ones in this chapter or ones you were reminded of) could be helpful to someone else in your life today? Take some time to send a verse or two to a friend in a text, email, note, or card. Not only will the other person be helped by this act, so will you as the writing of the verse(s) will again reinforce truth and right thinking in your mind and the soil of your soul.

Which of these verses do you need to write on a card or to-do list to come back to again tomorrow (and days again afterwards) for more reflection, prayer, and reframing of your perspective as to align your heart with His?

Exercises to do:

1. My favorite place to pray is in the woods or fields. (I wonder if this was the same for the Enoch of Genesis

chapter 5?) Walking helps me to receive wisdom, repent from sin, and return praise. So much so, that sometimes my husband asks me "Isn't it time for you to go to the woods?" after I've lashed out at him or someone else in a way that lacks grace, patience, or love. Keeping this idea in mind, consider setting aside an activity or two as a pathway to prayer – not just what might seem conventional. What about ironing or folding laundry (gratitude for these clothes, the ones wearing them, and the ability to do these chores from having equipment, electricity, and time)? Washing dishes or food preparation for cooking (gratitude for hot water, food to eat, and crying out for those who don't have access to these)? Carpooling or driving to work (gratitude for gas, a car that works, the people who ride in the car with you and learning of patience both from traffic and the people in the car)? Exercising or grocery shopping or… Seeing a chore as a pathway to prayer is an eternal way for truly making the most of multi-tasking. Breathe in that prayer and breathe out another one.

2. One of my friends taught me a great way to hold true to a promise that you would pray for someone. If someone asks you to pray for him, stop at that moment and pray with him. Yes, at that moment

-- whether you're in the grocery store, at the office, after class, on the phone, in the church hallway – now is always the appropriate time and place for prayer. Then, write the request down and pray again later. Better yet, follow these actions with number 3 on this list, if possible.

3. Have you ever received a thinking-of-you card? If so, can you remember how it made you feel loved or at least appreciated by someone else? You can do that and more for someone else with a praying-(or prayed)-for-you-today card. Something as simple as a little card with a Scripture verse and the date you wrote the card with a prayer for that person (or her family, church, neighbors, workplace, etc.) can be a powerful thing. This card is tangible evidence that God saw him in his need and prompted you to pray on his behalf. Take some time now to write a card or note while praying for someone. Then address it and mail it today, too. Then write his or her name in your calendar for today so you can be reminded to keep praying in faith, trusting God, and if God allows, one day, to rejoice with him or her in the answer to your prayers.

"*Where are you?*" (Genesis 3:9) questions for this chapter:

1. Does prayer ignite or intimidate your heart and mind? Do you see a need for prayer in your life today? Take some time to have a conversation with our Good God about your responses to those questions. Ask Him if He is satisfied with the topics your mind first goes to when you think about prayer.

2. To help you to keep focused in prayer, have you ever considered using the A.C.T.S. model? (A= adoration. C=confession. T=thanksgiving. S=supplication). Speak aloud or write down a point for each of these sections. Then consider going back through the model again or writing A.C.T.S. in your calendar for a later time today and again, tomorrow to return to our Good God in prayer.

3. Do you know someone whom you consider to be a "prayer warrior"? If so, see if you can schedule a meeting or phone call to discuss why prayer is so important to him or her. His or her thoughts on crying out could help strengthen and soften the soil of your soul to make prayer a bigger priority in your life for today and days to come.

Reflection prayer:

Dear Father God,

Thank You that You want me to talk with and listen to You in prayer. Thank You that You hear my prayers and answer with what You have as best. Thank You that You don't turn away or leave. Please help me to stop and listen to You more and more. Please help me to recognize and turn away from sin so that I might hear and obey You more and more.

In the strong Name of Jesus,

Amen.

[1]Foster, Richard J. 1998, "Celebration of Discipline: The Path to Spiritual Growth", Harper Collins, New York, NY. p. 33.

[2]Chambers, Oswald. 1988. *My Utmost for His Highest* daily reading excerpt flip chart, Garborg's Heart 'N Home, Inc., Bloomington, MN, reading for March 16.

CULTIVATING
CHARITY

*Let everyone give as his heart tells him, neither grudgingly
nor under compulsion, for God loves the man who gives
cheerfully. After all, God can give you everything that you
need, so that you may always have sufficient both for
yourselves and for giving away to other people. As the
scripture says: "He has dispersed abroad, he has given to
the poor; his righteousness remains forever."*
2 Corinthians 9:7 PHILLIPS

*"We seek to love [neighbors, creation, ourselves] as grateful
responses to the grace-filled fact that God first loves us."*
J.A. Nash[1]

Well Grounded

When I was growing up, my parents taught lots of students from all over the world. They were often in our home and us in theirs. I still remember my mother telling me before we went to one of our international friends' homes, "Now, Beth, remember – don't compliment them on whatever you see in their house." She said this, not to be mean or uncharitable in any way, but because she knew this truth: that if any of us said anything indicating that we liked something, they would package that thing up and we would be taking it home with us when we left that evening. They would, quite literally, give you the shirt off their back if they thought you needed it, or even just liked it.

Those international students lived with open hands and open hearts in love. Not always in a love from hearts knowing Jesus, but always in a love that reminded me of Jesus, then and now. A love that was lived out in a distinctive charity of giving.

I see that same charity in many of the international and missionary kid students today at my university. A distinctive charity of time, listening, interest, answering questions, vulnerability in language, and other gifts that cost them far more than the price of the gift itself. They give of themselves. In so doing, they challenge, convict, and compel me to do the same -- to give like Jesus, not just with them, but with others near and far.

They remind me of Jesus and make me want to live like He did. With open heart, ears, hands, and calendar for the person(s) in front of Him at that moment. He gave without expectation of return for His gift and without hesitation in the giving. He gave in love that was without limit. He was a living charity. His was a giving life.

Charity living is distinctive in its selflessness, for it is a life set aside unto Jesus. Charity living looks different from person to person, yet the same in pointing to the Person of Jesus. Charity living is developmental in its growth of a life reflecting the image of Jesus, both for the giver and the recipient. Charity living doesn't start or stop with charitable giving. It is a heart change resulting in a lifestyle that is distinctively different in its development of awareness and gratitude for the gifts all around us every day, along with the opportunity to be giving of ourselves to all in our world. With all that in mind, let's dig deeper into the concept of charity living through a life of giving.

As a Christian, my thoughts are naturally drawn to the Person of Christ in how my life should reflect His. As a soil scientist, my thoughts are naturally drawn to the world under my feet as examples of life itself. With all that in mind, could the ground itself in Eden have reflected the charity found in the Person of Christ? Its freely giving of water, nutrients, space, and suppression of disease and weeds[2] to nurture and sustain plant and soil microbial growth? Its continual giving out of help and taking in of waste? (Plants and soil microbes pump out waste materials in exchange for taking nutrients in from soil.) Its sustaining of the life in and above it?

If so, Eden's ground sharply contrasted with the ground outside it after the fall.[3] A now-cursed ground stingy or selfish in its giving and receiving, thus requiring work by Adam and his children for growing crops. Or as Genesis 3:19a ERV vividly puts it: *You will work hard for your food, until your face is covered with sweat.*

To dig a little deeper into the now-cursed ground concept, the soil was different than it was before the fall.[3] We can't know if the soil changed in composition, but we do know that it changed in cooperation. To apply this idea to people's lives, a change of heart has occurred.

Whether in Adam's day or now, it's only a change of heart that will change me into cooperating with Christ in charitable living. For it's only a change of heart that will make the soil of my soul into a fertile ground for the work of Christ to be made known to the nations (see Romans 12:1-2 and Matthew 28:18-20). Jesus wants my life to be full of Him. And if my life overflows with Him, it can be a tangible reminder of the beauty of Eden to all those around me living on this cursed ground today. But to have this kind of life, I need a heart that freely gives to others what is helpful, without expectation except that of receiving their waste of misplaced anger or rejection in return. I need a life that exudes the richness of a sustaining love that is always distinctive and often misunderstood.

We can see this principle clearly in 1 Corinthians 13:3 NASB: *And if I give away all my possessions to charity, and if I surrender my body so that I may glory, but do not have love, it does me no good.* To carry this idea a bit further, giving without love doesn't do anybody else any good either. This is not to say that God can't or won't use a loveless gift for good. Rather, the idea is that the gift's potential isn't achieved - what is a full belly or bank account if the recipient still feels unloved? Likewise, the giver is still lacking joy and hope if her motive in the gift is something other than love. Arrogance, guilt, or the desire for attention or distraction can never be satisfied or alleviated, no matter the size of the gift. This is because the giver is then left with what she started with – a hard, dry soul soil, barren and bereft of love's irreplaceable richness.

We can see this idea with Cain's gift in Genesis 4:3. He brought a gift of his crops to God, but Scripture suggests that it wasn't offered in worship, much less love. God rejected Cain's gift because He knew Cain's heart (see Genesis 4:4-8). Cain's subsequent anger and murder of Abel further delineate the difference between a have-to gift and a want-to gift.

Have-to gifts are obligations expecting returns from the receiver to the giver. A have-to gift really isn't a gift at all; it's a payment or a bill, depending on which way you consider it. In contrast, want-to gifts are delightful opportunities bringing joy to both giver and receiver. Having given and received both types of gifts, I know well what the presence (or absence) of love will do to a gift, independent of the size, type, or monetary value.

Let's take another look at our focal verse for this chapter to further dissect this idea - 2 Corinthians 9:7 AMPC:

> *Let each one [give] as he has made up his own mind and purposed in his heart, not reluctant-*

ly or sorrowfully or under compulsion, for God loves (He takes pleasure in, prizes above other things, and is unwilling to abandon or to do without) a cheerful (joyous, "prompt to do it") giver [whose heart is in his giving].

That *cheerful giver* is acting from love – both for her God and the one to whom she is giving. That love in her heart is from God, Who Himself is love (see 1 John 4:8). Or as the Jubilee version says – *for God is charity.* Charitable living happens because of God's Presence. For where God is, there is love/charity in its unmistakable richness of life (see entire chapter of 1 John 4).

And there in love's richness, little becomes much in and for the kingdom of God (see Matthew 17:20). Because in love's richness, the gifts are planned, purposeful, and penetrating to both the receiver and the giver (see Romans 11:29 and Hebrews 2:4). Also in love's richness, the gifts are good, just like those from our Good God (see Matthew 7:11).

For good gifts include:

1. Time in the listening, learning, and staying alongside in suffering
2. Talents and training in the advising, helping, problem-solving, and creating of beauty
3. Treasures in the supplying of stories, songs, laughter, money, and material objects

4. Truth-telling in the encouraging (without flattery), wisdom and knowledge bestowing, and gentle rebuking
5. Tenacity in the examples of faithful perseverance lived out over years and through yearnings
6. Testimonies in the day in and day out, seen and unseen choices of faith and hope
7. Tears in the giving, receiving, and sharing of compassion and grace

Wow! After writing this, I realized there were seven gifts in the list. Since seven is oft-considered a perfect number in Scripture, it was as if the alliteration itself wasn't enough of a good gift from my Good God today. It was as if He had to confirm it to me with a list of seven items for this number-loving soil scientist!

But when I stop and think about it, every idea, phrase, and word in this book is a gift I had to receive from my Good God. For a gift to be given, it must be received. This soil scientist isn't bright enough, much less good enough, to come up with anything worth being on a page; I only receive the ideas and words as a good gift, to in turn share with others.

As Christians, we are receivers of the very best gift ever – Jesus! His birth, life, death, burial, and resurrection can never be earned, only received (see Romans 3:23 and 6:23). His love, calling, Presence, and strength can never be purchased, only received (see 2 Corinthians 5:17; 21). Every day with Him is a want-to gift from Him to us; every day with Him can be a want-to gift from us to Him. When I choose to see my day like that, I choose charitable living in all the fullness of John 3:16 MSG: *This is how much God loved the world: He gave his Son, his one and only Son. And this is why: so that no one need be destroyed; by believing in him, anyone can have a whole and lasting life.*

And that's the kind of life I want today.

Cultivating Charity

Giving to others is our opportunity to express thanks to our Good God for all He's given us. We can never "out-give" our God, but we can easily "out-give" our-selves. Yet giving of ourselves opens us to see more of what God has given us. And when we see more of His grace in the gifts, we are freed to grace others with more of ourselves and what He has given us. Giving goes against self and displays God in ways that can't be dismissed or ignored by those who don't know Him. Giving opens both the giver and the receiver to a grace that points straight to God, the Giver of all good gifts. James 1:17 AMPC captures this so beautifully: *Every good gift and every perfect (free, large, full) gift is from above; it comes down from the Father of all [that gives] light, in [the shining of] Whom there can be no variation [rising or setting] or shadow cast by His turning [as in an eclipse].*

Take some time to look up, write out, and meditate on each of the Scriptures in this chapter, presented in order of appearance.

1. 2 Corinthians 9:7
2. Genesis 3:19
3. Romans 12:1-2
4. Matthew 28:18-20
5. 1 Corinthians 13:3
6. Genesis 4:3
7. Genesis 4:4-8
8. 1 John 4:8
9. 1 John 4
10. Matthew 17:20
11. Romans 11:29
12. Hebrews 2:4
13. Matthew 7:11
14. Romans 3:23 and 6:23
15. 1 Corinthians 5:17; 21
16. John 3:16
17. James 1:17

Questions to consider:

Which of these verses nourished the soil of your soul today with hope, joy, courage, or faith?

Did any of these verses remind you of other Scripture passages or stories which made you stop and think about the status of the soil of your soul? If so, then list the other passages or stories and their importance to your life today.

Which of these verses (the ones in this chapter or ones you were reminded of) could be helpful to someone else in your life today? Take some time to send a verse or two to a friend in a text, email, note, or card. Not only will the other person be helped by this act, so will you as the writing of the verse(s) will again reinforce truth and right thinking in your mind and the soil of your soul.

Which of these verses do you need to write on a card or to-do list to come back to again tomorrow (and days again afterwards) for more reflection, prayer, and reframing of your perspective as to align your heart with His?

Exercises to do:

1. Make a list of the top 3 gifts you've ever received from someone (excluding salvation). Include who gave you the gifts and why you chose these particular ones. Then make a list of the top 3 gifts you've ever given to someone. Now take some time to thank God for these gifts and the people involved in them, while asking Him for more opportunities

to give good and memorable gifts to others in your life today. Also pray for an increased love for all of the people who've come to mind while doing this exercise, along with an increased love for our Good God. You could include this as part of whatever activity you chose in chapter 6 to serve as a pathway to prayer.

2. Have you ever considered making a gift of the season for someone? To go outside and find beautiful leaves, grasses, flowers, branches, stones, bugs, feathers, fur, or soil samples. Pictures with your cell phone are also a great choice. And while you're collecting these items, pray for the one(s) with whom you're going to share these special pieces of beauty. Then assemble the items in a vase, box, bag, or a container made of the items themselves (think back to childhood days of making "pockets" from big leaves or tying together small sticks with twine or vines – please don't worry if they're lopsided or droopy, because physically many of us are too in some way(s)!). Take or send this gift with a note to the one(s) for whom you prayed while collecting them. Also, if you have enough materials, make one for yourself to put in a place where you'll see it and be reminded to watch for opportunities to give of yourself in time, talents, training, treasures, truth-telling, testimonies, or tears.

3. Have you ever thought about giving to the earth itself? A gift of resource conservation in gratitude and worship of our Creator God? Consider making a list of ways you can save natural resources in your everyday life – turning off the lights when leaving a room, carpooling or combining errands into one trip, raising the thermostat in summer or lowering it in winter, shorter showers, eating in-season and local foods purchased at a farmer's market or home grocery, going vegetarian for a day (or two), and so many others. Be creative and purposeful in your choices for conservation, always keeping your heart and mind fixed on our Good God Who created and sustains all of this and us too.

"Where are you?" (Genesis 3:9b) questions for this chapter:

1. What gives you the most joy to give to someone? Gifts of time, listening, hugs, or tangible gifts? Does this type of gift reflect your own love language or theirs? If you don't know about love languages, google Gary Chapman and *The Five Love Languages* to learn more about this. And if you do know about them, ask God to bring to your mind one person needing a gift from you today that's in his or her own love language. (A great place to start is with a spouse, child, neighbor, or student.)

2. Consider making giving a regular part of your week through drawing or inserting an icon of a gift-wrapped box into your calendar as a prompt to be looking for someone on the fringes of your life who needs love in a tangible way. Is it the person you see on the side of the road on the way to work or school? Is it the person who fills your order at the restaurant or empties your trashcans or delivers your mail or some other often-overlooked task in your daily life? You don't have to know someone's name to bless them in the Name of Jesus. He knows each person's name and need. You might be the one He sent to meet that need today or tomorrow.

3. Even if you are already pretty good at giving to others, how are you at receiving from them? Rank how you feel about receiving help, gifts, compassion, and such from others from between 1 ("I won't") to 10 ('bring on all the gifts"). Take some time to put these ideas and yourself before God to learn from Him how charity needs to change in your life, for yourself and for others in your life. Something to reflect on: when you joyfully receive a gift from someone else, you give him the gift of joyous giving. And from personal experience, that gift of joy is a most lovely thing!

Reflection prayer:

Dear Father God,

Thank You that You gave Jesus for me. Thank You that You keep giving strength, hope, and faith to me. Thank You that You are the giver of all good gifts. Thank You that You will teach me how to give good gifts to others in Your love. Please remind me that nothing can separate me from Your love and that nothing can change You or Your love. Please help me to love You more and to love others like I love myself.

In the strong Name of Jesus,

Amen.

[1]J.A. Nash, *Loving Nature: Ecological Integrity and Christian Responsibility*, 1991, Abingdon Press, The Churches Center for Theology and Public Policy, Nashville, TN, p.141.

[2]Granted, neither disease nor weeds might have been present in Eden before the advent of sin – I'm just including these for a broader thought on the many contributions that a charitable soil would make for plant growth.

[3]Yes, the ground in location was now different post-fall, since Adam is no longer in Eden. But looking back at Genesis 3:18-19, I think we could assume the ground itself was different than it was previously from having received the curse from sin.

CULTIVATING CONSTANCY

But you must keep on being strong to take trouble. Then you will be all right in every way. You will not need anything more.
James 1:4 WE

But let endurance and *steadfastness* and *patience have full play* and *do a thorough work, so that you may be [people] perfectly and fully developed [with no defects], lacking in nothing.*
James 1:4 AMPC

"My grandparents made sense of living [in rural South Carolina] by a hearty Baptist faith, which gave thanks for the land's bounty, and bounded greed by gratitude to the Creator, and pride to the indebtedness to the blood of the Lamb."
W. Jenkins[1]

Geologists refer to soil as "merely" or "just" weathered rock. They often dismiss it as that layer needing to be moved before getting to the good stuff of the rocks buried below. Needless to say, when this soil scientist heard soil described like that in the geology classes I took in college, my internal response was to want to buck up and say "NO sir, soil is FAR more than that!" Thankfully, my common sense and teeth didn't let my tongue take over with my real reaction to those misinformed words.

My visceral response to the weathered rock statement lasted far beyond college and graduate school. It wasn't until the past few years when I saw this geology concept in a whole new way. A way that related directly to my life lived out day after day as a Christ-follower in the dust of today. And to think of this way in terms of a question in the theme of this book: could there be a deeper relationship between the dust, soil, and Adam of Genesis 2 and us as the *living stones* of 1 Peter 2:5 ESV?

After saying all that, yes, soil is weathered rock. A soil's inorganic particles of sand, silt, and clay have formed from the aging and decay of its parent material, rock. Different types of rock make different types of soil. Therefore, a soil can vary in its chemical and physical composition because of the type of rock(s) it formed from. As importantly, the amount of time, type of climate, topographical location, and organisms present near or in the rock directly impact the soil formed because of their interactions with the rock. (Keep in mind, organisms include us humans.)

But soil is not *just* weathered rock. It is a waste-receiving, nutrient and water-giving, life-supporting entity comprised of *formerly* rock and living, carbon-based organisms, which are working together for others to thrive in and from them. Both the rock-weathering and organism life and death processes are essential for soil to become what it is, so that many can get life from it.

As Christians, we are commanded to see Jesus as our Rock and Redeemer while living lives reflecting Him as *living stones* (see Psalm 19:14 and 1 Peter 2:5). Also, as Christians, we are instructed to hold fast to the Stone the builders rejected while setting memorial stones in our lives to remember what Jesus has done in and for us (see Luke 20:17 and Joshua 4:7). Moreover, we are to be changing into His Image while He molds our lives into being good soil for the 30-, 60-, 100-fold harvest of Matthew 13:23. Thank You, Jesus, for giving us a *heart of flesh* for a *heart of stone* (see Ezekiel 36:26 ESV)!

Keeping those ideas from geology, soil science, and Scripture in mind, I know that I must undergo death and weathering for my stony life to become good soil. For as a Christian, my Christ, the Rock, lives in me, not I (see 1 Corinthians 10:4 and Galatians 2:20). Every day should be a removal (a weathering, if you will) of what is not me, to reveal what is me, my Christ, the Rock alive in me. To apply geological thinking here, each day is a process to make me into that *living stone* comprised of the Holy Spirit in my biological body, actively transforming me into Christ's Image for God's glory and the good of His people.

Jesus longs for my life to be good soil. A soil that is rich in nutrients of love, grace, mercy, and patience, so that others around me might see the Rock on which I stand and be drawn to Him to gain what is needed for their own lives (see Psalm 40:2). Thus, as a Christ-follower, my *living stone* life should be nothing more than weathered rock or nothing less than good soil.

To recap, rock weathering involves the interactions of time, climate, landscape position, and biota with the bedrock itself. Different rock types respond in different ways to these factors and their interactions. For example, a "hard" rock like granite or basalt will experience far less measure-able weathering with exposure to any or all of these factors than a "soft" rock like mica or limestone. Thus, a soft rock will be more easily made into a nutrient-rich soil. For this reason, soils from soft rocks can be good sources of plant-essential nutrients for crops growing in them. A classic example of this idea is the limestone-based soils in the bluegrass region of Eastern Kentucky. They are famous for raising those long-legged Thoroughbred racehorses, who have big needs for calcium, magnesium, and other nutrients for good bone development.

Two principles can be seen here: (1) circumstances put into my life by my Good God are key to the development of good soil in my life; and (2) if my heart is soft towards my Good God and His work, then good soil development in my life should be faster and more useful to others around me.

Looking back to the previous example about Eastern Kentucky bluegrass soils, if the limestone bedrock were present in an area without its relatively warm, wet climate, receiving a good measure of solar radiation, then the limestone might not decay into being such good soil for healthy Thoroughbreds. Similarly, if my life isn't exposed to the grief, pain, and loss of suffering, I might not become good soil for the work of God. In other words, suffering can be the soul-forming factor for me to become the *living stone* and good soil I should be. God can use suffering to transform my life into a richness of Christ-likeness that nourishes others with responses of grace, patience, mercy, constancy, and love. And at least for this soil scientist, suffering has been and is a most influential soil-forming factor in its decay of my arrogance and self-sufficiency. (Trust me, there's still LOTS of weathering that needs to happen to my rock-hard pride, but my Good God is both gracious and relentless in His work in my life – hallelujah!)

Constancy is a lifestyle of *trusting obedience* learned from suffering (see Hebrews 5:8 in the Message version. And while you're there, be sure and take some time to revel in the idea that Jesus learned this way too). Constancy is a distinctive quality of one choosing a *living stone* life, day in and day out. Constancy is that day after day life of consistent choices reflecting an unwavering trust planted deep in the soil of my soul that He alone is my Good God and Rock forever. King David captured this idea in Psalm 31:3 NIV: *Since you are my rock and my fortress, for the sake of your name lead and guide me* and Psalm 61:2 KJV: *From the end of the earth will I cry unto thee, when my heart is overwhelmed: lead me to the rock that is higher than I.* Constancy isn't easy or shiny, but is always worth doing and produces worship.

Constancy is not a giving-up or giving-in, but a giving-out. Jesus gives out love, faith, and hope to me. I can then give out these to others. A giving-out of joy for strength, hope for despair, and beauty for ashes planted by God deep in the soil of a soul seeking Him in the suffering. Elisabeth Elliot said it best when she said, "Accept it…And that is the key to peace".[2] For the *living stone* sufferer knows well that she would quickly decay into the defeat of self-absorbing pity without holding hard to His Presence, purpose, and plan as good. She also knows well that this decay would not be into good soil but into a dead, dry dust full of denial and defeat. (And take it from this soil scientist, dead, dry dust "don't do nothing for nobody" other than make them choke and cough on their own arrogance and anxiety.)

Dust – that layer every housekeeper wants to remove, as it is nothing more than a pointing-finger reminder of what once was (rock) and no longer is (soil). Yet when considered in light of Scripture, dust becomes far more. And suffering can also be far more in the life of a *living stone* believer (see

Genesis 2:7). For as God breathed life into dusty Adam, He can transform the dust of today into a joy alive with hope.

Because without Christ alive in me, I am but dust, body and soul. This truth becomes especially evident in suffering. Psalm 73:26 EXB captures this idea with: *My body and my mind [heart] may become weak, but God is my strength [the rock of my heart]. He is mine [my portion] forever.*

For in the life of a *living stone* Christ-follower, suffering will come. When the dust-bowl winds of suffering come, constancy will be the first piece of good soil in my life to erode, if I am not being held together by my Jesus, my Rock (see Colossians 1:15-17). For after constancy erodes, faith, trust, and resolve can quickly follow and be blown away forever.

The constancy of *trusting obedience* of Hebrews 5:8 requires far more than dust can give; it depends on Christ alive in me, constantly showing me that He is that *living hope* (1 Peter 1:3). That hope that doesn't disappoint reminds me there is much good to be unearthed through trusting God in the dust of this weary body and soul in this day (see Isaiah 49:23 NIV). And this hope gives courage, strength, and endurance to keep standing firm amidst a world crumbling around and in me (see Ephesians 6:10-17).

Yet when Christ is there, trusted, and taken for His word in constancy by a Christ-follower in suffering, everything changes. And those changes are as distinctive as comparing rock to soil.

The living component of a soil is essential for the soil to support and sustain life far beyond its physical boundaries. The plant, animal, and microbial populations in soil perform functions that nourish today's crops and tomorrow's seeds. They change waste into fertilizer, untie bound nutrients, create pathways for growth, and change the soil environment in ways far beyond our understanding.

Similarly, the impact of our lives as *living stones* being used as the *good soil* of Matthew 13 can extend far beyond our physical, mental, and emotional boundaries. Because with Christ alive working in and through us, constancy can be a distinctive lifestyle. Our constancy in prayer and patience, giving and going, and devotion to Christ while denying self can evangelize and disciple many in our lives. Everything in our culture tends towards quick and easy solutions, which often don't work for the long-term. Yet constancy in trusting God as Good with the now and not-yet is the only sustainable answer for hope and help for us, the world, and the cursed ground we live on.

There are so many in our world mired in the mud of the everyday. Constantly choosing to trust and know my God as Good cultivates hope. And hope cultivates joy and love, especially when I'm stuck between a rock and a hard place. For when I put my hope in my Rock and Redeemer, I am given eternal perspective that lasts far beyond the pain of this dusty day. And in that eternal perspective, I can see how those seemingly small choices of constancy -- of obedience even when no one is looking, prayer, worship, confession and repentance, giving, selflessness, and other marks of a Christ-follower -- can bear huge harvests of mustard-seed faith (see Matthew 17:20). And those mustard-seed faith harvests can not only move mountains, but can change rock-hard hearts into soft soil for the good work of our Good God, who is our forever Rock (see Isaiah 26:4). Because in suffering, there is none other besides, before, or behind our Rock (see 1 Samuel 2:2). Thanks be to God, our Rock!

The LORD is my solid rock, my fortress, my rescuer.
My God is my rock— I take refuge in him! — he's my shield,
my salvation's strength, my place of safety.
Psalm 18:2 CEB

Cultivating Constancy

Cultivating constancy isn't a one-time choice or commitment. It's a daily, if not minute by minute, opportunity to follow Christ and trust Him and His plan as good. It's making those choices that show Christ as my one true love and choice, no matter what comes along, including suffering. It's getting up and doing the next task as unto Christ, no matter how I might feel about the task. It's being there and believing truth, even and especially when it hurts. It's keeping my mouth shut on complaining (and open in silent prayer) when the situation isn't to my liking. It's deciding that the other person's honor or recognition is more important than mine. And lots of other choices that point to my Good God, instead of to myself.

And when suffering comes into the picture, cultivating constancy to keep on trusting God as Good in all things can require more strength than I have or can dig up. Yet that's the hidden beauty of constancy – that God gives the joy for strength when I have nothing left to give. So, if you're in the midst of a dust-storm of hard life circumstances, now is the time to press in even harder to our Good God, the Rock Who doesn't change or turn away in any way, no matter what happens (see Psalm 55:19).

Take some time to look up, write out, and meditate on each of the Scriptures in this chapter, presented in order of appearance.

1. James 1:4
2. 1 Peter 2:5
3. Psalm 19:4
4. Luke 20:17
5. Joshua 4:7

6. Matthew 13
7. Ezekiel 36:26
8. 1 Corinthians 10:4
9. Galatians 2:20
10. Psalm 40:2
11. Hebrews 5:8 (in the Message version)
12. Psalm 31:3 and 61:2
13. Genesis 2:7
14. Psalm 73:26
15. Colossians 1:15–17
16. Hebrews 5:8
17. 1 Peter 1:3
18. Isaiah 49:23
19. Ephesians 6:10–17
20. Matthew 17:20
21. Isaiah 26:4
22. 1 Samuel 2:2
23. Psalm 18:2 and 55:19

Questions to consider:

Which of these verses nourished the soil of your soul today with hope, joy, courage, or faith?

Did any of these verses remind you of other Scripture passages or stories which made you stop and think about the status of the soil of your soul? If so, then list the other passages or stories and their importance to your life today.

Which of these verses (the ones in this chapter or ones you were reminded of) could be helpful to someone else in your life today? Take some time to send a verse or two to a friend in a text, email, note, or card. Not only will the other person be helped by this act, so will you as the writing of the verse(s) will again reinforce truth and right thinking in your mind and the soil of your soul.

Which of these verses do you need to write on a card or to-do list to come back to again tomorrow (and days again afterwards) for more reflection, prayer, and reframing of your perspective as to align your heart with His?

Exercises to do:

1. Do you have a favorite rock or rock collection? If not, then now is the time to start. If possible, go outside and find one or more neat-looking or neat-feeling rock(s). If needed, clean it off with soap and water using a stiff brush (unless it's a very soft rock that flakes easily – then use a soft rag.) You might also need to soak the rock(s) overnight in soapy water for better results. If you can't go outside to get a rock, consider using aquarium or decorative rocks (those

used with potted plants or vases). Then, put the rock(s) where you are working on this study or where you regularly study your Bible so you can see it and be reminded of your life as a *living stone* Christ-follower. Next, choose a Bible verse (either from the ones here or one that you already know and cherish) and write it on piece of paper to put with your rock. (Or write or paint the verse directly onto the rock itself. Rocks and Scripture are beautiful in and of themselves. Thus, there's no need to worry about being artistic or using fancy handwriting in putting on a verse.) If you're anything like me, you would benefit from having a rock with a verse in multiple places in your home or office for constant reminders that our Good God is our Rock Who never changes. And you might like to do what I do at times, to carry around a little rock in my pocket as a tangible reminder of the constant and unchanging Presence of God as my Rock and Redeemer. I can put my hand in my pocket and feel the cool smoothness of the rock, which somehow seems to remind my heart that God is with me and that He is good, no matter what my day might look like. It's almost as if touching that rock in my pocket reminds me yet again of the need to choose to praise my Rock Who created the rocks and me too for His purpose for today and the not-yet.

2. If you've never written out your story (or it's been a while since you did), consider taking some time to do this as a new challenge to use it (or parts of it) in your everyday life with others for pointing to Christ as the Rock Who is unchanging in power and position and Presence for you and who can do the same for them. Please don't leave out, downplay, or ignore those parts of your story involving suffering. Those portions of your story which involve suffering can be especially powerful and heartening to someone else living in hard circumstances. Pieces of how God brought you (or is bringing you) through suffering in His strength (and not yours) can be as little rocks of encouragement to someone else needing to hear of His provision and His goodness in the everyday. Every person's story is worth telling and telling often! You can never know how God might use your story for His plan; ask Him for the courage to tell your story and for the opportunity to tell it. You don't have to be fancy in words or know all the answers. You just need to rely on God to provide what is needed, when it's needed. Now is the time to tell of Him and His great love for all of us. So, whenever you see a rock, let it serve as a prompt to be looking and praying for another time and another way to share your story with someone new in your life. Your story could be a

stepping-stone to our Savior for someone you already know or haven't met yet!

3. While we're on the subject of rocks, consider creative ways you can incorporate rocks into your daily life as a means of reminding you of the need to cultivate constancy in your walk with Christ and others. Rocks remain; we need to do the same with our trust and finding hope in God. Thus, putting a rock in view or in touch can be a tangible way to remind us to remain faithful to God, our Rock as He always is to us. What about: giving a vase of flowers with stones as the base to a friend living in hard life-circumstances; going to an elderly or ill family member or friend's home and redoing their flower garden by removing weeds and setting up weed prevention with rock (or mulch) installation; buying cards or stationery with rock images for sending encouragement notes; or whatever else our Good God brings to mind. Please remember that when God puts something in your mind to do for someone else, it's the right thing and the right time (even if it might sound outlandish or odd to you). So do it and watch and expect the goodness of God to be displayed to the one for whom you're doing it and to yourself in the process.

"Where are you?" (Genesis 3:9b) questions for this chapter:

1. In looking over your past week, how would you rate yourself for constancy, with your words lining up with your actions and both of them lining up with your faith in God? It's easy to say "Yes, I believe that"; it's not easy to actually make choices that reflect what you've said you believe. And then to probe a bit further, how does your constancy of words and actions reflect your faith in our Good God to provide what is needed, when it's needed? Use two or three adjectives to describe how you'd feel if you were someone else on the receiving end of your words and actions about constancy.

2. Now, take those words and do one of the following with them: present them in a prayer of thanksgiving for them in God's provision of your being constant as unto Christ-likeness in word and action; offer them in supplication to our Good God for continued growth in constancy for the coming week; or release them to our Gracious King as a confession of your need for His strength to prevail in your life, for radical change reflecting the importance of constancy in your everyday choices. If the words you chose in question 1 aren't ones you'd like to use to describe a life of constancy, what three words do you wish *did* describe your choices

in constancy? If possible, write one or two of these words in your calendar on at least two or three days in this month and the next to serve as a reminder for the importance of cultivating constancy in your pursuit of Christ-likeness in your life for today and the not-yet.

Reflection prayer:

Dear Father God,

Thank You that You are always faithful, even when I'm not. Thank You that You don't change, even when You want me to. Thank You that You persistently and patiently want to teach me more about Your great and steadfast love for me. Please help me to value the need and the importance of being constant in choosing to trust You as Good in all ways and all things, even during suffering. Make my soul soft like limestone, that the weathering of life will be effective in me. Please help me to keep on keeping on in learning to love You and Your ways and Your will.

In the strong Name of Jesus,

Amen.

[1]Jenkins, W. 2008, "Ecologies of Grace: Environmental Ethics and Christian Theology, Oxford University Press, Oxford, England. P. 26.

[2]Elliot, Elisabeth. 2018. *Suffering is Never for Nothing*. B&H Publishing Group, Nashville, TN, p.51.

CULTIVATING
CHARACTER

I have been crucified with Christ [in Him I have shared His crucifixion]; it is no longer I who live, but Christ (the Messiah) lives in me; and the life I now live in the body I live by faith in (by adherence to and reliance on and complete trust in) the Son of God, Who loved me and gave Himself up for me.
Galatians 2:20 AMPC

"True Christlikeness, true companionship with Christ, comes at the point where it is hard not to respond as He would."
D. Willard[1]

If you're anything like me, a big plate of good pizza or onion rings can make you downright happy. That pizza or onion rings doesn't need anything else to cause me happiness and a full stomach, except for maybe a nice, cold soft drink or milkshake with which to wash them down. And both are even better shared with friends, aren't they? That is, provided there's plenty of pizza and onion rings to go around (word to the wise: do not come between this girl and her food).

If needed, you have my blessing to leave now and go and get that good pizza or onion rings, or better yet, both! They are scientifically proven brain-foods which will not only quiet growling stomachs, but help brain neurons to fire more rapidly for making more and faster connections for learning. (Or at least this soil scientist likes to believe that [big grin]!) Then we can sit back down again and feast together on good foods for our stomachs, minds, and hearts as we continue in this chapter.

Did you know that both the best tomatoes for pizza and onions for onion rings are only grown in one place in the world? These places are San Mateo, Italy for San Mateo tomatoes and certain counties in Georgia, USA for Vidalia onions. Yes, you guessed it! This phenomenon is because these varieties of tomatoes and onions only thrive in the soils present at these specific locations.

The exclusive combination of properties of these soils are uniquely ideal for the cultivation of these specific vegetable varieties, promoting their distinctive characteristics of sweetness, texture, juiciness, color, abundance, and timing of ripeness. This is because the soil-forming factors of parent material, biota, climate, time, and topography have produced the perfect nursery-soils in Italy and Georgia for the tomatoes and onions, respectively. Other soils can support the growth of these vegetables, but not like the soils in San Mateo or Georgia. That distinctive tang, color, and size of the tomato or that special sweetness and fleshy texture of the onion can't be duplicated when grown in any other type of soil.

These characteristics are definitely missed when not present. Missed not just by a select group of foodies, but by (most) anyone who has that taste, look, or texture of the San Mateo tomatoes or Vidalia onions imprinted on their tongues and brains, yearning to savor the happiness found in the first bite that lingers long after the plate is clean.

Similarly, the distinctive characteristics of a Christ-follower are present only when his or her heart, mind, and soul have been planted in the soil of *agape* love, grace, and mercy found solely at the foot of the Cross. Nearness, love, grace, and mercy are essential minerals for the distinctive characteristics of trusting obedience, faith, and humility to thrive in a Christ-follower's life. Thus, a Christ-follower's growth in the soil at the Cross will yield a character uniquely known as one who is dead to and for herself, but alive through and with Christ. If Christ's character is present, His characteristics will be evident in his or her life, no matter the location, time, circumstances surrounding, or physical condition of the Christ-follower.

Every encounter -- or taste, if you will -- with this kind of Christ-follower points back to the place where she was planted and is being grown. Those Galatians 5:22-23 ESV Spirit-fruits of *love, joy, peace, patience, kindness, goodness, faithfulness, gentleness,* and *self-control* can't be duplicated or replicated. The taste of Spirit-fruits is unmistakable when present and irreplaceable when absent. This holds true no matter what other attractive attributes might be on the table that day in conversation, choices, connections, or companionship. A life distinctive in the character of Christ, and thus, Spirit-fruits, only flourishes in a soul's soil when it is rich in the unique composition of Christ-likeness minerals of nearness, surrender, grace, mercy, and love.

And that's the kind of characteristic life I want today and for whatever days are yet to come. Not just because I've tasted and eaten days filled with less than this, but because I want to be distinctive as one who carries the unmistakable mark of Christ. I long to be one who brings plates-full of Spirit-fruits to others in front of me and outwards from there. I yearn to be that salt of the earth of Matthew 5:13, leading straight towards growth in faith in the One Who never leaves or stops loving, no matter what I do or where I am (see Hebrews 13:8). I want to model the One Who lets me remember my sins while gently reminding me that He has forgiven all of them, thus cleansing me all the way down to the last particle of the soil of my soul (see Isaiah 1:18).

With all of this in mind, this soil scientist can't help but ponder more on grace, mercy, and character in this chapter. Please know I'm not putting anything forth as theologically foundational, but rather as spiritually inspirational in how it's drawn me closer to our Good God in the asking and thinking through of questions, with the hopes it might do the same for you.

Since I don't have the brainpower to even begin to understand any of these gloriously beautiful and distinctive truths about character, love, and a distinctive life, this is a feeble attempt to grasp even one particle of them. Scripture tells me that grace calls me to delight in forgiveness and freedom forever, knowing that my sins are gone *as far as the east is from the west* (Psalm 103:12 ESV). Scripture also teaches me that mercy lets me remember my sins while reveling in the knowledge that Christ has paid for them *once for all* and welcomes me over and again when I return to Him in repentance (Romans 6:10 ESV and see 1 John 1:9). Thus, my receiving of His grace and mercy prepares and sustains me for growth in a soil of vigorous faith rich in praise, prayer, and powerful obedience. Similarly, my rejecting of His grace and mercy leaves me denying my sins of pride and unbelief, which produce not only a deficit of hope in my life but in others' lives also. For if I believe my past, present, or future are either good enough or beyond redemption, I am deceived by the lie of "I got this" which erodes a thin topsoil of faith, exposing a bedrock of fear.

Unfortunately, I know all too well that a life based on fear is very different in character than one based on Christ. A character of fear is distinctive in anger, bitterness, impatience, selfishness, greed, jealousy, and other such traits contrary to Christ-likeness. And these characteristics are only magnified when one possessing them is in stressful situations where temptation can reign. That bedrock of fear brings out the worst in even the best of us, doesn't it?

John Wooden captures the idea of the true value of character with, "the true test of a man's character is what he does when no one is watching."[2] Or in the words of this soil scientist, character is what you really are in the soil of your soul. I want nothing other than Jesus implanted and infused in every particle of me, and since you've hung on this long in the book, I think you want the same. David talked about this yearning in Psalm 84:10 CEB: *Better is a single day in your courtyards than a thousand days anywhere else! I would prefer to stand outside the entrance of my God's house than live comfortably in the tents of the wicked.*

Scripture has many distinctive characters in its scope – those who lived in faith and those who didn't, including Cain as seen in Genesis 4. Cain's life (and likeness) were marked by sin's selfishness in ways that God and others could see, even if he did his best to hide it (see Genesis 4:15). For even there in the sin, God's grace-giving left a mark on Cain's head for all to see and to know distinctively and instinctively that Cain was still His and always would be. (Thank You, God, that

You still claim each and all of us as Yours, no matter whom we've murdered in our thoughts or wounded with our words! Thank You for such powerful love and glorious grace!)

Abel's murder was but one display of Cain's character, as evidenced in a reading of Genesis 4. This thought makes it even more fascinating to me that it's only after the birth of Adam's grandson, Enosh, where we see a true change in character in the children of dust – *At that time people began to call upon the name of the LORD* (Genesis 4:26 ESV). Could this timing reflect that Adam and his descendants via Seth had then started to learn the fundamental differences of the character of a life formed by fear versus that formed from faith? They'd tried to live on their own on cursed ground and all the fears implicit in the curse and failed miserably. Could they have realized then that they couldn't truly live by their own strength? This idea could be evidenced by the steady decline in righteousness until God reset humanity via the flood, the ark, and Noah's family in Genesis 7.

Noah was distinctive in his choices to obey God despite circumstances and culture. He chose to obey God in all the details, directions, and distinctiveness of: building an ark; loading up animals, food, and family; drifting along until the dove returned with a branch; consecrating and starting over on new land; and believing God in the rainbow promise. And I'm betting that there's a whole lot more to this story than we can read about in Scripture, requiring Noah to hold out a strong mustard-seed of faith to God, day after day. On that note, if you've still got any pizza or onion rings left (or even if you don't), now is a great time to stop and savor a slow, out-loud read-through of Noah's story in Genesis chapters 5 through 9.

Noah hadn't lived in perfection before the flood, unlike Adam did in Eden. Yet both Noah and Adam had to start life over in a brand-new land. A new land possibly familiar in shape and form but probably fearful in its differences from what they knew before flood or fall. Both farmers were tasked with feeding their families using now-unfamiliar resources of soil, water, nutrients, climate, and other factors beyond their control. Talk about having to start from the ground up! Situations like these require character deeply rooted in faith like Scripture described of Noah in Genesis 6:9 and 22 and 7:5 ESV: *He was a righteous man, blameless in his generation. Noah walked with God* and *he did all that God commanded him.*

I do want to do all that God commands me to do, but many times my want to obey Him doesn't exceed my want to order my own life. Adam's lie of "my way is better" too many times rings louder in my heart and life than the truth of finding freedom in the path of obedience to Christ (see Psalm 119:32). You'd think I'd have learned by now with all the dismaying and disastrous data I've collected from repeated disobedience that the hypothesis of "I got this" doesn't work. But nope. Yet, thanks be to God for grace! He didn't give up on Adam, Cain, David, or so many others in Scripture. And that gives me such hope – hope that maybe today will be the day that the soil of my soul will start changing into being distinctively like Christ, with a richness in the essential minerals of nearness, humility, grace, mercy, and love. That my character might start bearing Spirit-fruits in a life uniquely planted with mustard-seeds of faith, which glorifies God and compels others to taste and see that our God has been, is, and always and forever will be good (see Psalm 34:8).

Cultivating Character

Just like all the growth that must occur under the soil surface before the first green plant shoot appears, character development is essential for health in all ways. I can only fake being good at or in something for a short time until the truth takes over. Likewise, with character, I can only do (or try to do) what is right for a little while before my true character takes over anything I've been trying to replicate out of a sick or stunted growth of character. As the British would say, "the truth will out". Every. Single. Time.

Cultivating character requires me to choose "what would Jesus do?" in any and every situation, whether or not people see me doing it. God sees. God knows. And that's all that really matters. Do I try and make myself look good in telling only part of the truth? Do I think of others before thinking of myself in doing something? Do I swallow back a rude, self-righteous, or rough answer and extend grace to another in conversation? (After all, grace is undeserved in and of itself. Plus, I'm already the recipient of MUCH grace (see Ephesians 2:8-9). And so are you.) Do I make good choices in what I watch or listen to, even when no one else is around? That old adage of "garbage in, garbage out" is always true and applicable. Do I work as unto God in my job, with my family, for the environment, and whomever God puts in front of me each day (see 2 Timothy 2:15)? And these are just a few examples of the questions I need to ask myself daily in the continual pursuit of cultivating character in my own life. Has our Good God brought any other questions to your mind for your life while reading my list? If so, consider taking some time to write them here in the margins, in your calendar, on your refrigerator or bathroom mirror, or anywhere you can see them as a prompt to pursue Christ-like character in all aspects of your life, starting today.

Take some time to look up, write out, and meditate on each of the Scriptures in this chapter, presented in order of appearance.

1. Galatians 2:20
2. Galatians 5:22-23
3. Matthew 5:13
4. Hebrews 13:8
5. Isaiah 1:18

6. Psalm 103:12
7. Romans 6:10
8. 1 John 1:9
9. Psalm 84:10
10. Genesis 4
11. Genesis 4:15 and 4:26
12. Genesis 5-9
13. Genesis 6:9; 22
14. Genesis 7:5
15. Psalm 119:32
16. Psalm 34:8
17. Ephesians 2:8-9
18. 2 Timothy 2:15

Questions to consider:

Which of these verses nourished the soil of your soul today with hope, joy, courage, or faith?

Did any of these verses remind you of other Scripture passages or stories which made you stop and think about the status of the soil of your soul? If so, then list the other passages or stories and their importance to your life today.

Which of these verses (the ones in this chapter or ones you were reminded of) could be helpful to someone else in your life today? Take some time to send a verse or two to a friend in a text, email, note, or card. Not only will the other person be helped by this act, so will you as the writing of the verse(s) will again reinforce truth and right thinking in your mind and the soil of your soul.

Which of these verses do you need to write on a card or to-do list to come back to again tomorrow (and days again afterwards) for more reflection, prayer, and reframing of your perspective as to align your heart with His?

Exercises to do:

1. God set the rainbow in the sky as a promise to Noah that He would never flood the earth again. We can use that idea today with cultivating character. Let's consider using a rainbow as a reminder of the need and opportunity to always be seeking Christ-likeness in our daily life choices. Every time you see one, let it serve as a prompt for you to reflect on your character, and how closely (or not) it lines up with Christ. With that in mind, here's a best-case scenario – it's just finished raining and you can see a rainbow – go outside and revel in it now by reading aloud Genesis 9:8-17, while letting the soil of your soul cry out to our Good God to help you grow in Christ-like character today. Be sure and take a picture of the rainbow while you're out there too. But if you don't

have the tangible gift of a rainbow in your world right now, it's time to make one. Draw a picture of a rainbow. Bring out all the crayons, markers, and colored pencils and delight in the doing of this as an act of worship to our Good God Who always keeps all of His promises. Then consider how you can use this drawing to bless someone else who is struggling in his or her faith today – write his or her name on the picture with the date and commit to pray for him. Then pin up this picture somewhere you can see it every day to follow through on your promise to pray. As we've said before in this book, a commitment (and a follow-through) on the discipline of prayer is one of the very best ways to cultivates closeness with our Good God and in turn, character.

2. Go to biblegateway.com or another Bible search engine. Type in the word "promises" and go through the list of what comes up, all the while looking for promises you need now to help your character to grow more Christ-like. We need to know the promises to know how we need to grow to be more like our Christ. Promises of faithfulness, love, help, and so many others can challenge us to not become satisfied with what we are but to keep striving to look forward to our Christ. Read aloud those promises which speak deep truths to the soil of your soul. Then write out 1-3 of these promises

to return to later for more strengthening of your faith. Then consider memorizing these promises to reinforce the desire for growth into Christ-likeness.

3. Humility, a vital facet to Christ-like character, is found in Philippians 2:3ERV: *In whatever you do, don't let selfishness or pride be your guide. Be humble, and honor others more than yourselves.* With that in mind, consider purchasing or preparing a meal for someone you know who needs to taste and see that our God is good today. Lots of people have only encountered pride or selfishness from those calling themselves Christians. They need tangible acts of service done in loving humility to counteract that stereotype. Such people who probably come to mind first are those with sickness or grief/loss, but you aren't limited to this group. Food can be a feast that reaches far past doubt or fear into the heart of one rejecting faith in seemingly all ways. And the sweet taste of grace lingers long after the food is gone. This same principle holds with using whatever gifts our Good God has placed into our lives to grace others. Do you love sewing, pottery, painting, or other handcrafts? What about making something for someone or teaching someone how to do a craft? Car or home repairs? Playing music? Gardening in the sharing of vegetables, fruits, flowers, seeds, or advice? Styling, braiding, cutting or coloring hair?

Organizing or cleaning out closets? There's almost as many different ways to serve others as there are people. Now is always a great time to display God's beauty in your talent and time for someone else. But if you're one who does love to cook, craft, garden, etc., bring out all the things you need to make your best gift for the one(s) God has impressed upon your heart for today or tomorrow (or calendared for a specific date very soon).

"Where are you?" (Genesis 3:9b) questions for this chapter:

1. Write out Galatians 5:22-23. Then circle the Spirit-fruits from this list which you see actively displayed in your life today. Take a minute or two to thank God for the work He is doing in your life today to build Christ's character in you.

2. Look at Galatians 5:22-23 again. Write out 1-3 Spirit-fruits which need nourishing in your life today. Take some time to ask God to show you what is needed in your daily routine for vigorous growth of these fruits in your life.

3. If you wrote down a question or two earlier for your life in response to my list, go back and write down

some "action points" where you can implement these ideas in your routine today and again tomorrow.

Reflection Prayer:

Dear Father God,

Thank You that You alone have and give what is needed for any and every situation, including the strength to make Christ-like choices. Thank You that You want me to be more like Your Son in all ways. Please help me have the faith of Noah and to obey You even when it seems easier not to choose Christ-likeness. Please help me to listen only to You and ignore the lies trying to drown out the truths You've implanted in the soil of my soul. I want to be more like Jesus; please help me do this every day.

In the strong Name of Jesus,

Amen.

[1]Willard, Dallas. 1988. "The Spirit of the Disciplines: Understanding How God Changes Lives", Harper San Francisco, Harper Collins Publishers, New York, NY. p. 8.

[2]https://www.forbes.com/sites/walterpavlo/2012/10/23/character-is-what-you-do-when-everyone-is-watching/?sh=29cf4c67fc6d

CULTIVATING
CREATION CARE

*O LORD, our Lord, how majestic and glorious and
excellent is Your name in all the earth! You have displayed
Your splendor above the heavens.*
Psalm 8:1 AMP

*"By the sweat of your brow, you will produce food to eat
until you return to the ground, because you were taken from it.
You are dust, and you will return to dust."*
Genesis 3:19 GW

*"Human necessity is not just to know, but to cherish and
protect the things that are known, and to know the things that
can only be known by cherishing…they must be pictured in
the mind and memory…'by heart' so that in seeing or
remembering them the heart may be said to 'sing'."*
W. Berry[1]

One of my very favorite gifts ever came from one of my very favorite students ever. It has sat in its place of honor in my office for some years now and isn't going anywhere anytime soon. This gift is one that always makes me smile, not just in thinking of that student, but in the love, empathy, and creativity wrapped up in it.

By now, you're probably asking, "what's the gift?" Well, it's a small jar of soil my student collected from her family farm. She gave the jar to me with these words: "Dr. Madison, I wanted to give you something extra special and I couldn't think of anything that you might like more than soil I took from my family's farm just for you." Let me tell you – she was so right in knowing this soil scientist's heart. To me, that's tangible love in a jar with the lid screwed on tight!

As a farm girl, my student knew the principle of placement better than most do at that age. She and I used to talk about how we felt most like ourselves when we were on our family farms. We shared in the deep satisfaction of being able to point to a specific place of *adamah* ("fertile earth") and thus, to know the implicit beauty contained in the idea of *from the ground... to dust* alluded to in Genesis 3:19 ICB.

Dust to dust isn't reserved for funerals or failures. *Dust to dust* is pieces of Eden which stick under fingernails and to pants while seeping into the soil of the souls working with it. *Dust to dust* is an irreplaceable part of every day for one who knows the vitality of working with the land and its inhabitants, be they microbes or mountain ranges or all of us kept in-between. *Dust to dust* points to that which is of and from us and leads us closer to the One who made it and us, too.

With these ideas in mind, could God have intended for the principle of *dust to dust* for Adam and for us to be another reminder of His placement of us, His purpose for us, and His permanence towards us?

His placement of us – God's choice is for good for each of us in this place and in this position, wherever He has put us. I may not see the good in the dust of the here and the now, but I can trust Him. He is Good and the giver of good gifts (see Genesis 50:20 and Matthew 7:11). Therefore, whether or not I see this dust of me and around me as good, it is good because it is from God.

His purpose for us – God had purpose for Adam in and after Eden. He has purpose for each of us here living from dust to dust. As the first Adam's offspring, we have inherited Adam's obligation as caretakers of creation. As the second Adam's co-heirs, we have received redemption and renewal so that we might fulfill this responsibility of caretaking our Good God's creation in and around us (see 1 Corinthians 15:45 and Romans 8:17). As caretakers, we must remember that our responsibility includes soil, seeds, and stars for today, with souls as our primary focus for eternity.

His permanence towards us – This God is the same God Who has always been and always will be (see Psalm 15:4 and Hebrews 13:8). The same God Who formed Adam from dust and does the same for each of us, before we are known by any other (see Genesis 2:7 and Psalm 139:13-16). The same God mighty in power, rich in love, and steadfast in keeping all of His promises (see Deuteronomy 3:24, Exodus 34:6, and Joshua 21:45). The same God Who is oh so much more beyond understanding or imagination (see Ephesians 3:20-21)!

Not all of us are called to be environmental scientists, but all of us are commissioned to be creation's caretakers. We have been given access and authority for everything from soil to stars as stewards of the Most High God (see Genesis 1:28). None of this is ours in ownership, but all of this is ours to answer for in our actions towards it. John Stott refers to creation care as an important characteristic of Christian discipleship that's "often neglected and yet deserve[s] to be taken seriously."[2]

Here is where you probably expect me to bring out terrifying statistics like: over 99% of our world's freshwater supply is contaminated; estimates of thousands of species of plants, animals, insects, reptiles, and fish have already gone extinct; or that most of our landfills are full and leakage from them is not only seeping into our soils but also our groundwater supplies. Trust me, I could go on and on to fill up far more than just one book with much more nightmarish data than this, collected from every part of our planet.

Yet one foundational truth resounds strongly through and in all of this seemingly hopeless chaos in our seemingly out-of-control world. God (repeatedly) called His creation good when He made it and hasn't said otherwise (see Genesis 1). He reinforced this idea of good about the created throughout Scripture with the words and work of kings and kinsmen, prophets, priests, psalmists, scholars, shepherds, and the Savior Himself, just to name a few. (This soil scientist likes that kind of data with every piece and particle of her being!)

Even the strongest of us sometimes cannot help but be blown to and fro as dust in the winds of change and uncertainty. But as Christ-followers, we know nothing can begin to move our God. Nothing can stand before our God, including the dust of today, which tries to choke us in materialism, arrogance, apathy, and discontent (see Deuteronomy 7:24, 2 Chronicles 20:17, and Ephesians 6:11). All or any of these sins can easily erode faith into fear. And when we hold fast to fear instead of trusting God in faith for all of this, we become cowards of creation rather than caretakers of it (see Proverbs 3:5-6). For example, if I am focusing on the data telling me that all is already lost with the world's resources, I am limiting God to what I can measure, understand, or control. Similarly, if I am reckless or selfish and without concern as to resource availability and wise usage, I usurp God in believing the lie that I am owner of creation, not its steward. Then, I have deceived myself. Because there in fear, I am not living *from dust to dust*; I am living only for me, myself, and I.

Please hear me – I am not pointing a finger at anyone --except myself--in any of this. I know far too well the sins

I have committed as an apathetic, arrogant, and discontented rejecter of my assigned role as a submissive steward of creation. More importantly, I know our Good God to be loving, patient, and kind in extending powerful grace and mercy that transforms once for all and once forever (see Hebrews 7:27). Only He can restore hearts and homes and lives and landscapes, all scarred with sin's ravages. Nothing and no one is beyond His reach and redemption for now or the not-yet (see Psalm 139:7-12). He created and called it good in Genesis. He sustains and calls it His own today. Just as He gave Adam opportunity to do good in Eden, He does the same for me here. And He alone can give the strength to choose faith over fear (see Joshua 1:9).

Fearing the *dust to dust* of creation requires that I keep a chokehold of dominion over it. Faith in the One Who made me as *dust to dust* releases me to find the beauty in creation and to care for it with hope, joy, and courage. Fear demands understanding and control. Faith delivers freedom to run in the path of obedience, even and especially when I don't understand everything seemingly out of control in or around me (see Psalm 119:32). (Only faith speaks louder than data to this scientist.) For example, fear of the future will cause me to orient my daily choices around that which I can control in resource availability – providing for me and my own here and now, no matter the cost to others living now or in the future. In contrast, faith opens my eyes to see that God has purpose and plan for those now and those to come in their resource needs. Thus, I can joyfully make good choices for resource conservation because I know that He can, does, and will provide what is needed (see Psalm 104:28 and 145:16).

Every day I can make good choices for resource conservation, such as adjusting my thermostat, carpooling or combining errands, cold wash and air-dry laundry, running full dishwasher and laundry loads, eating local produce or vegetarian, buying stock in green technology research and development companies, thrifting clothes and household items, and so many others. These choices may not make significant impacts on global resource availability, but the doing of them can draw me closer to my God in obedience. The repeated small surrenders of my will for His glory and the good of His people can reorient my days into deeper worship of Him through a growing awareness of the *dust to dust* of His creation. And there in worship is where this dusty woman needs to stay each and every day.

At the risk of sounding too earthy or spiritualistic, even the physical act of walking the fields or woods at my family farm can be a reaching back to Adam and forward to those yet to come. The names and memories of those I knew and loved are more vivid there amidst the trees, soil, rocks, and stream than in picture frames or photo albums. The legacy of all of Adam's children of dust swirls up around my heart and mind like the fog of early morning in creek bottomland and reminds me that my Good God remembers that I am dust too (see Psalm 103:14).

That reminder fills the desolate spaces of the wasteland mentality of "me against the world" while pushing back against the lie of "I will never be enough." This is because Adam's legacy in us is evidence of our relentless and persistently Good God, Who loves without change or end and gives mercies made new every morning (see John 3:16. 1 John 3:1, and Lamentations 3:22-23). And every morning is when I need a fresh reminder of this legacy and my Loving God's Presence with me, no matter how dusty the day might seem. So I often take a walk to try and clear a path through the dust of fear clouding my heart and mind as a reset into the proper perspective of faith.

A good walk in those woods or fields resets me to return to my Creator in these ways:

1. A joining with my neighbors in work, worship, and witness of all that God spoke into being at creation and has sustained every day since then (see Genesis 1 and Deuteronomy 11:11-12).

2. A symphony of praise, petition, and humble position with all my living and non-living neighbors in creation, groaning in expectation of the revealing of the last days (see Romans 8:19-22).

3. A holy act of recognition that God has purpose in and for all of whom He's created in the dust of today (see Ephesians 2:10).

4. A confession of my forgetting the need for a right perspective of my place here between pre-fall Eden and the coming new heaven and earth, with a

renewing of hope that today is one piece of eternity yet to come (see Genesis 1 and Revelation 21).

And then and there, the soil of my soul is finally ready to call back to my God with a deeper cry for shalom for all of us living here from *dust to dust* (see Isaiah 26:3).

Shalom isn't just the absence of war; it's the fullness of a peace that reaches down from God to and through me and out to my neighbors. My neighbors range from people to plants, microbes to marsupials, and the soil to the stars. Living and not, God created us to abide together in shalom with Him in the perfection of Eden and the dust of today. Shalom might be an unachievable ideal globally, but personal obedience isn't. I am responsible for cultivating shalom through caretaking creation in whatever ways God puts in front of me. Big or small, caretaking choices require deliberate and diligent surrender of my desires, just like all other choices to take up my cross and follow my Christ (see Matthew 16:24). Or as God Himself said, *love your neighbor as yourself* and *do to others as you would have them do to you* (Leviticus 19:18 ESV, Luke 6:31 NIV).

The best way for me to know how to love my neighbor(s) is to better know my God Who made all of us and calls us to live with Him in shalom. Only He can give the courage, hope, wisdom, discernment, and resolve to keep finding the *strength for today and bright hope for tomorrow* necessary for joyously living from *dust to dust* (see hymn lyrics for *Great is Thy Faithfulness*[3] and Ephesians 1:18-20).

Cultivating Creation Care

In case you haven't already realized it by now, there's so much more I could say on this. With that in mind, I hope that you've kept your eyes and mind wide open during this chapter (and all the other chapters too, of course!) to new ideas and the need for growth. Not just growth in practical, every-day choices of tangible things, but more so, growth in that which is eternal: a spiritual yearning for intimacy with our Good God through His books of Scripture and nature, both as His child and as appointed caretaker for all that resides in your world. Let's keep our hearts and minds seated in His lap, gazing at His face in adoration while our hands and feet do His good work in all and for all He sets before us today.

Take some time to look up, write out, and meditate on each of the Scriptures in this chapter, presented in order of appearance.

1. Psalm 8:1
2. Genesis 3:19
3. Genesis 50:20
4. Matthew 7:11
5. 1 Corinthians 15:45
6. Romans 8:17
7. Psalm 15:4
8. Hebrews 13:8
9. Genesis 2:7

10. Psalm 139:13-16
11. Deuteronomy 3:24
12. Exodus 34:6
13. Joshua 21:45
14. Ephesians 3:20-21
15. Genesis 1:28
16. Genesis 1
17. Deuteronomy 7:24
18. 2 Chronicles 20:17
19. Ephesians 6:11
20. Proverbs 3:5-6
21. Hebrews 7:27
22. Psalm 139:7-12
23. Joshua 1:9
24. Psalm 119:32
25. Psalm 104:28, 145:16, and 103:14
26. John 3:16
27. 1 John 3:1
28. Lamentations 3:22-23
29. Deuteronomy 11:11-12
30. Romans 8:19-22
31. Ephesians 2:10
32. Revelation 21
33. Isaiah 26:3
34. Matthew 16:24
35. Leviticus 19:18
36. Luke 6:31
37. Ephesians 1:18-20

Questions to consider:

Which of these verses nourished the soil of your soul today with hope, joy, courage, or faith?

Did any of these verses remind you of other Scripture passages or stories which made you stop and think about the status of the soil of your soul? If so, then list the other passages or stories and their importance to your life today.

Which of these verses (the ones in this chapter or ones you were reminded of) could be helpful to someone else in your life today? Take some time to send a verse or two to a friend in a text, email, note, or card. Not only will the other person be helped by this act, so will you as the writing of the verse(s) will again reinforce truth and right thinking in your mind and the soil of your soul.

Which of these verses do you need to write on a card or to-do list to come back to again tomorrow (and days again afterwards) for more reflection, prayer, and reframing of your perspective as to align your heart with His?

Exercises to do:

1. Make a list of all the natural resources you've used in the past hour. Be sure and stop to think outside

the box on this list – you might be surprised at what you find in pondering. Now rank these resources in order of importance to your daily life. Then rank them in order of your gratefulness for them being available to your daily life. If needed, stop and think about your response the last time the electricity went out at your house, office, or church – was it frustration or anger? Use those emotions to further cement thankfulness into your day.

2. Take a walk around your house, office, or church and make a list of how you could be better caretaking creation here today. A few ideas to get the juices of awareness and excitement flowing include: installing automatic thermostats, raising thermostats in summer or lowering in winter, washing on cold and air drying laundry, only washing full laundry or dishwasher loads, turning off the faucet while you're brushing your teeth or the lights/TV/radio/etc. when you leave a room, composting, intentionally eating leftovers or freezing them for later, eating vegetarian choices or locally grown produce, thrifting, giving, or sharing clothes/linens/furniture/appliances/etc. This exercise isn't meant to make you feel guilty but rather ready to receive more grace in the form of obedience in often overlooked stewardship opportunities.

3. If possible, set aside time to go on a walk with God outside – leave the electronics at home or turned on silent. This walk isn't for exercise; it's for removing vestiges of entitlement as to reorient your mind, heart, and life from the mindset of ownership to stewardship. Smell the air. Feel the breeze on your face. Touch the green around you in at least three kinds of plants. Notice the blue or gray of the sky against and with the clouds. Hear the animals/birds/water/trees/wind around you. Feel the soil and rock underneath you with your feet and then with your hands. Let these experiences activate gratitude which will lead you into worship – not of creation itself, but of the Creator God Who is there with you and longs for you to know Him more even now. And then even more again the next time you walk for worship with all of creation singing in joy around and with you!

Consider making step 3 a regular part of your week. Having a journal to record what you hear from our Good God during these times is a great way to reinforce thankfulness and humility towards Him and all the neighbors He has placed in your part of the world today and however many days yet to come.

"Where are you?" (Genesis 3:9b) questions for this chapter:

1. Have you felt tired lately of hearing stuff about protecting the environment? Or frustrated in *not* hearing about the need for creation care? If so, write a couple of descriptive words in the margin about your thoughts. Then, take some time to seek God in prayer for extra patience, both with others and yourself in your concerns about this topic.

2. What fears do you have about living in the mindset of *from dust to dust* in your everyday choices in creation care? Be honest – our Good God knows all about these fears even better than you do, and He loves you just as you are, fears and dust and all.

Reflection Prayer:

Dear Father God,

Thank You that You spoke all of this around and in me into being and called it good. Thank You that You have always had purpose for each neighbor and for me in this place and in this time. Thank You that You give strength for today and hope for tomorrow, even in the dustiest of days amidst the dustiest of people like me. Please help me to see more like You do – to see beauty and worth in the overlooked, and opportunity in the forgotten or rejected. Please help me to capture every word and every action for caretaking of Your creation, for Your glory and the good of Your people. Please help me to overcome my fears with the faith You give – thank You for such a strong love that never gives up on anyone, including me.

In the strong Name of Jesus,

Amen.

[1]Wendell Berry in *This Sacred Life: Humanity's Place in a Wounded World*, N. Wirzba, 2021, Cambridge University Press, Cambridge, UK, p. 33.

[2]Stott, John. 2010. *The Radical Disciple: Some Neglected Aspects of our Calling*, IVP Books, InterVarsity Press, Downers Grove, IL. p. 16.

[3]https://hymnary.org/text/great_is_thy_faithfulness_o_god_my_fathe, as accessed on 3/17/23.

CONCLUSION

Because God knows how we're made,
God remembers we're just dust.
Psalm 103:14 CEB

"The creation of human beings out of dust is presented as an
inexplicable, inextricable, and wonderful process."
C. Westerman[1]

G od blessed me with parents who have modeled a
well-grounded life to me for 55 years now. They
continue to show me how to love God, people, and all of
creation well in the rhythms and routines of everyday life.
They put feet to the gracious humility and mercy seen in the

depiction of Jesus found in Philippians 2:7 AKJV: *but [he] made himself of no reputation, and took upon him the form of a servant, and was made in the likeness of men.* They see the best in people because they see God as He is, as Good.

Mother finds beauty in the present and the simple in her home, just like Daddy does in his garden. She practices intentionality in: getting out the fancy silver, crystal, and china for guests; following a recipe to the Nth detail every single time; picking up lint off the carpet or off that sweater set; taking out a missed stitch and starting over on anything, including dishtowels; and the like. Even though I grumbled in my mind (and under my breath as a teenager), I learned not just how to do all the things, but the why of doing them. Colossians 3:23 EXB explains this concept well with: *In all the work you are doing, ·work the best you can [do it heart and soul; from the soul]. Work as if you were doing it for the Lord, not for people.* Both Mother and Daddy taught me that doing something from the soul was to capture the beauty of this moment and to bless the One Who made this task, moment, and me from the dust.

As both Mother and Daddy would say to me (or anyone, for that matter), "don't look at me, look at Jesus." And that's exactly what I hope you've found in this book – glimpses of the beauty of a life lived for the glory of Christ and the good of His people. This moment, this task, this place, this person in the mirror and in front of you is beautiful because our Good God has made all of them. Each and every one made for His glory and the good of His people living here in a dusty world. Each and every one offering us glimpses of Eden and eternity if we will stop and look for beauty in the present and the simple (see Psalm 34:8).

For when I stop to look, I see His love in the details and the design. I see His grace in the doing and the declaring. I see His mercies in the hidden and the heartbreak. I see His joy in the marveling and the making. These only hint at and beckon to the much-more my eyes and mind can't begin to comprehend of the soil under my feet and in my soul.

And the not-understanding is beautiful in and of itself, for it reminds me that I'm not the one who made or keeps any of this. Rather, I'm the one given opportunity to worship and work for the One Who did. For the One Who did is the same One Who welcomes my questions, no matter how many and paltry they are. The One Who then takes my questions and shows me more of Himself, Who calls me to a greater knowing of Him through seeing and delighting in more of His creation.

I say this only as one (very) slowly learning of the beauty of and need for meeting with my Jesus in the present and the simple of this day made by Him and for Him (see Psalm 118:24). Those choices requiring stopping and silence, listening and looking pull back arrogance's curtain of lies and help me see past the dust of myself and into the deep love of Christ (see Ephesians 2:4 and 1 John 3:1). For Christ is the One Who knows me better than I know myself and loves me still (see Psalm 139:13-16). And He does the same for and with you even now, no matter how dusty you may feel.

No matter if you've read every word, answered every question, or written out every verse contained in this book and many others (or not), you can't earn His love (see Zephaniah 3:17, 1 John 3:16 and 4:16). No matter if you've set up the best resource conservation plan, budget, or calendar in your home, office, school, and church (or not), you can't buy His mercies (see Lamentations 3:22-23). No matter if you've always been the one who did all the things at all the times and in all the ways for all the people (or not), you can't deserve His grace (see Ephesians 1:6 and 2 Timothy 1:9).

No one can.

Not even Adam before the fall could earn or deserve even one particle of that love, mercy, or grace. Therein lies the real beauty of the present and the simple. God gives His love. God gives His mercies. God gives His grace. We receive the mercies and grace as good gifts from our Good God (see Matthew 6:33 and John 15:7). We receive them as people of dust living from *dust to dust* in the freedom and security of knowing that He *remembers that we are just dust* (Psalm 103:14 ESV). And there's nothing more beautiful and joyful than knowing that truth and living that truth here in the dust of today.

None of what we've explored in this book is especially enjoyable, much less easy, to let the Holy Spirit implement in our lives. But the change that any and all of these disciplines can bring to our lives is essential for growth towards our Good God and for more to enter His kingdom here on earth and for eternity. We have been tasked as caretakers

Conclusion

of all of creation, from soils to stars to souls. Thus, it is our opportunity for worship to become more like Christ in the doing of such good work while looking back to Eden and forward to the new heaven and earth yet to come. May it be known that as we work and worship our Good God in the doing, our dusty hearts cry out with the rest of creation, *So, Lord Jesus, please come soon!* (Revelation 22:20 CEV).

Take some time to look up, write out, and meditate on each of the Scriptures in this chapter, presented in order of appearance.

1. Psalm 103:14
2. Philippians 2:7
3. Colossians 3:23
4. Psalm 34:8
5. Psalm 118:24
6. Ephesians 2:4
7. 1 John 3:1
8. Psalm 139:13–16
9. Zephaniah 3:17
10. 1 John 3:16 and 4:16
11. Lamentations 3:22–23
12. Ephesians 1:6
13. 2 Timothy 1:9
14. Matthew 6:33
15. John 15:7
16. Revelation 22:20

173

Questions to consider:

Which of these verses nourished the soil of your soul today with hope, joy, courage, or faith?

Did any of these verses remind you of other Scripture passages or stories which made you stop and think about the status of the soil of your soul? If so, then list the other passages or stories and their importance to your life today.

Which of these verses (the ones in this chapter or ones you were reminded of) could be helpful to someone else in your life today? Take some time to send a verse or two to a friend in a text, email, note, or card. Not only will the other person be helped by this act, so will you as the writing of the verse(s) will again reinforce truth and right thinking into your mind and the soil of your soul.

Which of these verses do you need to write on a card or to-do list to come back to again tomorrow (and days again afterwards) for more reflection, prayer, and reframing of your perspective as to align your heart with His?

Concluding *"Where are you?"* (Genesis 3:9b) questions:

1. How have you seen growth in the soil of your heart and life since participating in reading and learning from Scriptures contained in this book? Has your appetite for spending time with and in worship of

our Good God changed since incorporating in your life the types of questions explored here?

2. What do you plan to do in coming days to help combat living in the defeat or dustiness of the routine of just making it through another day or to-do list? What measures have you put into place to help you be more aware of the beauty around you in neighbors, places, time, and tasks?

3. What did you learn from the Scripture contained in this book that will help you love your neighbors as yourself and love your God with all your heart, soul, mind, and strength?

4. What practices did you encounter in this book which you'd like to incorporate into your daily rhythms and routines as to cultivate intimacy with our Good God?

Concluding Exercise:

Consider taking some time to pray and ponder the implications of the lessons learned. Take some time to review the chapters which spoke most clearly to the soil of your soul. Also, consider taking some time to pray for yourself and your role as caretaker of all aspects of creation (including those people you see in the mirror, your home, office, or neighborhood). Take some time to ask our Good God for a greater awareness to see more beauty and thus, opportunities for service, submission, and supplication in worship of our Good God.

Reflection prayer:

Dear Father God,

Thank You that You always want me to come closer to You. Thank You that You want me to become more and more like Jesus every day. Thank You that You keep showing me love, grace, and mercy. Please help me want to be more like Jesus every single day. Please give me a heart that keeps looking for ways to love You and Your people more today and then again even more tomorrow.

In the strong Name of Jesus,

Amen.

[1]Westerman, Claus. 1994. *Genesis 1-11: A Continental Commentary*. Fortress Press, Minneapolis, MN, p. 205.

AFTERWORD

But the fruit of the Spirit [the result of His presence within us]
is love [unselfish concern for others], joy, [inner] peace,
patience [not the ability to wait, but how we act while
waiting], kindness, goodness, faithfulness, gentleness,
self-control. Against such things there is no law.
Galatians 5:22-23 AMP

—»—‹‹—

Dear Reader,

I wish I could say the picture you see here is a picture
of my garden. Sadly, it isn't. However, it is a picture of one
of my neighbor's gardens down the road from my family
farm. Yet this picture is a prompt for me to pray for abun-

dant growth of the Spirit's fruit in my heart, that my life might be a good garden for the work of my Good God.

What makes this picture especially beautiful is that every type of vegetable is flourishing. The rows are lush in leaf and thick in that which is coming soon to someone's dinner table. (I wonder if this picture could be a glimpse of what Adam knew in Eden before the fall? If so, then he sure ate well!) The garden's purpose is to nourish with nutrients for healthy bodies and lives, for this generation and those to come. The above-ground portion is for today's tables, while the below-ground portion stores organic matter in the soil for future tables. To this soil scientist, that kind of beauty is both distinctive and desirable. A beauty that nourishes with nutrients for body, spirit, and soul. Not just to hold body and soul together, but to move spirit closer towards the shalom found in seeking the fullness known only in the Presence of our Good God.

That outpouring of shalom flourishes in the rich soil of a soul set aside unto Christ and bears a rich harvest for those for whom it is farmed. Hebrews 6:7 (PHILLIPS) captures this idea with: *Ground which absorbs the rain that is constantly falling upon it and produces plants which are useful to those who cultivate it, is ground which has the blessing of God.* Since you've made it this far in the book, I think you're like me in wanting good ground which has the blessing of God to be made manifest in the garden of your life too. Frequently when I look out across grounds rich with abundance like my neighbor's garden and the hay fields and forests of my family farm, I find myself saying "please, God, I want my life to look like that." And I keep praying that same petition over and again because I know this: God can and will do the impossible (see Luke 1:37). He is not limited by my past mistakes, present fears, or future unknowns. He is not confined by circumstance, condition, or my lack of cooperation. Jeremiah said it best in chapter 32, verse 17, part b (AMPC): *Nothing is too hard* or *too wonderful for You.*

I need that truth from Jeremiah to soak deep in the soil of my heart like a good rain and then for it to grow more seeds of faith and nourish joy for strength (see Nehemiah 9:10). And those faith seeds are evidence of these truths:

1. Only God can take the little of my trying and make it into the much of His triumphs over temptation or trial.
2. Only God can transform what seems over in today's failures into what is overcoming in tomorrow's hopes.
3. Only God can translate what I can't understand into what He wants to use as evidence of His glory.

Honestly, I want the wonderful without the work. But many times, God's growing of good gardens in my life demands lots of work, and lots of hard work at that. If you've done any gardening at all, you know vigorous vegetables only result from a constant working against unwelcome and unwanted weeds and other pests. And I've found the same to be true for Spirit-fruit in the garden of my heart.

Incorporating the spiritual disciplines into our daily lives opens eyes and hearts to discovering more and more beauty, which feeds a hunger for a harvest of more Spirit fruit. This incorporation isn't easy or simple. But its effects are surely prominent in today's harvest of peace and patience and promised in the one-day-coming's harvest of people and pearls (see Revelation 21).

This book, the *Good Ground* series, and other books coming soon from Northeastern Baptist Press (NEBP) are my today's harvest of the hard work of incorporating the spiritual disciplines into my life, especially that of prayer. That little setting-aside of five minutes as sacred listening has morphed into far more over the years. Prayer has become a near-constant conversation with my Good God (see Philippians 4:6-7). He hasn't ever turned me away (and won't) with one–too many questions or requests, which is saying a lot for this stubborn soil scientist (see Hebrews 13:5). Instead, He stoops to listen, love, and lead one step at a time (see Proverbs 3:5-6). And trust me, if He will do this for me, He will do it for you and in ways far more than you can ask or imagine (see Ephesians 3:20-21).

For more ideas and encouragement for taking that next step towards abundance in the garden of your life, please consider purchasing other books from NEBP and following my blog at soulscientistblog.com. I'd love to hear from you about how our Good God works in your life and others' lives in ways that are beyond your asking or imagining!

Gratefully,
Beth

Explanation of pictures in this book

O Lord, You have always been our home.
Psalm 90:1 GNT

Lord, You have been the place of comfort for all people of all time.
Psalm 90:1 NLV

All the pictures you've seen in this book are of my family farm (except the afterword, which is from our neighbor's garden). This farm is the physical home where my heart and many generations of hearts before me have resided. This piece of ground that's come from our Good God's provision still feeds hungry bellies and hearts with bounty and beauty, as it's done for over 150 years now.

(And hopefully it will continue to do so for many years to come!)

Yet the true legacy of this farm is my knowledge of God as my heart's home, no matter where I live or what happens in my life. My parents and grandparents taught me that bounty only comes from the hard work of hands and hearts put to God and ground at the plow and in prayer. Such work carefully cultivates gifts seen by the eye and known by the soul. Gifts like these include clean consciences and clear water sources, green fields and a growing faith, and rich soils under our feet and in our souls. These gifts require my caretaking with daily diligence and determination to remain on my knees in humble worship of my Good God. Only He is worthy of nothing less than adoration and acceptance of my role as child and caretaker of all He has made. He has given much; I am responsible for much (see Luke 12:48).

Thank You, Jesus, for this ground and this grace. I believe in You to keep providing the strength to trust You to care for this land and these longings to know You more. Please help me find the wisdom and wonder known only in abiding in Your Presence and peace.

Dr. Madison and her granddaughter

ABOUT THE AUTHOR

Dr. Beth Madison has received a B.S. in Plant and Soil Science from the University of Tennessee, a M.S. in Soil Conservation from the University of Kentucky, and a Ph.D. in Soil Microbiology from Kansas State University. She currently teaches at Union University, and has previously taught at South Georgia State College, Western Kentucky University, Kansas State University, and University of Kentucky. She has nearly twenty-five years of experience in teaching soil, plant, and environmental sciences, and nearly twenty years of teaching Bible studies to various audiences ranging from youth to senior adults. You can read more of Beth's writing at *soulscientistblog.com*.

Also from Beth Madison
and Northeastern Baptist Press:

Good Ground
Volumes 1 and 2

-->>- -<<-

In both volumes of *Good Ground*, Dr. Beth
Madison examines the Christian life through a
unique lens. Just as Jesus' parables used agriculture to communicate spiritual truth, Beth uses
soil science to celebrate God's amazing creation
and encourage a healthy, growing walk with Jesus. *Good Ground* volumes 1 and 2 will enhance
your daily devotions and small group studies.

Good Ground
~ Volume 1 ~

B

Good Ground
~ Volume 2 ~

Beth Madison

www.ingramcontent.com/pod-product-compliance
Lightning Source LLC
Chambersburg PA
CBHW031509120626
46545CB00005B/1805